AF516361

Caste and Race

Caste and Race

Comparative Study of
BR Ambedkar and Martin Luther King

MOHAN DASS NAMISHRAY

RAWAT PUBLICATIONS
Jaipur • New Delhi • Bangalore • Guwahati • Kolkata

ISBN 978-81-7033-787-4
© Motilal Bhimraj Charity Trust, 2003

Reprinted, 2017

No part of this book may be reproduced or transmitted in any form or by any means, electronic or mechanical, including photocopying, recording or by any information storage and retrieval system, without permission in writing from the publishers.

Published in association with
Motilal Bhimraj Charity Trust
732, Modern Society, Sector 15, Rohini, Delhi - 110 085
Phone: 2729-8589 E-mail: bharatj@nda.vsnl.net.in
Website: sanatanadharma.net

Published by
Prem Rawat for **Rawat Publications**
Satyam Apts., Sector 3, Jawahar Nagar, Jaipur - 302 004 (India)
Phone: 0141 265 1748 / 7006 Fax: 0141 265 1748
E-mail : info@rawatbooks.com
Website: rawatbooks.com

New Delhi Office
4858/24, Ansari Road, Daryaganj, New Delhi 110 002
Phone: 011-23263290

Also at *Bangalore, Guwahati* and *Kolkata*

Typeset by Rawat Computers, Jaipur
Printed at Chaman Enterprises, New Delhi

Contents

Preface

A variety of development programmes launched for the advancement of the scheduled castes since independence have not *ipso facto* improved the social and economic conditions of a majority of dalits. Plannings and plan-makers are on hot lines. Publicity is carried on day and night. One can easily hear the slogans to improve the pathetic condition of downtrodden communities in India. These fundamental issues have been debated and pondered over by us for some time. The same kind of situation can be found with respect to blacks in America.

This is a comparative study on dalits and blacks. In spite of not wishing to, I have used the word 'negro' at some places, especially as many of the writers quoted here have made use of the term. In India, for instance, the word 'Harijan' has been used for years. I have, however, given preference to the use of 'black' in place of 'negro'. I am grateful to Motilal Bhimraj Charity Trust that has financially helped me in this work, Bharat Jhunjhunwala, who has made an immense contribution to this endeavour by way of incisive discussion which sharpened my views on the subject and Mrs. Vidya Bhaskar for editing the manuscript. I am also indebted to Centre for Developing Social Studies and American Library, New Delhi where I consulted many valuable books, and met the senior fellows, who guided me on the concerned subject. The portraits of Dr. B.R. Ambedkar and Dr. Martin Luther King used on the cover were provided by Sri Shant Swaroop Baudh and American Library, Delhi respectively, for which I am thankful to them. I again acknowledge with thanks the cooperation and assistance provided by Motilal Bhimraj Charity Trust towards completing the research.

Mohan Dass Namishray

1

Race Relations: The American Context

A study of social relations, as personal relations, between members of different races or race relations, necessitates, at the outset, a clear understanding of what is meant by ethnic groups and the meaning of race and racial conflicts. A historical review of race relations points to racial antagonism as having its genesis in modern times: it developed, and racial segregation was reinforced, with the discovery that the natives, 'the coloured peoples', could easily be economically exploited by the Europeans especially with the growth of capitalism in Europe and America. The practice of slavery was racial exploitation at its crudest, with the slaves, without disguise, treated like animals. It is interesting to observe different aspects of the social status and family life of the slaves and the relation between the master and the slave: for instance, inter-racial sex relations and the emergence finally of the accommodated slave, who defined his existence in terms of his servitude. Modern race relations are concerned with the economic and social status of the whites and the blacks, their inter-marriage, their classification—into one group or the other—owing to mixed blood, as well as the basic ideological problem for whites in altering their relationship with the blacks as reflected in the white liberalism trend of the post-1960s.

What do we mean by 'social relations' and how do we define liberty, analysing the system of equality of opportunity for the blacks and the whites in American society?

'Social relations' here refers to personal relations between men and not to the whole range of relations between men implied by the ordinary scientific usage of the term. 'Liberty' in the context of social equality is, strictly speaking, a kind of 'social' liberty than 'personal' or individual, which is what is emphasised by Myrdal when he talks of racial discrimination: "it must be left to the individual white man's own discretion whether or not he wants to receive Negroes in his home, shake hands with them and eat with them."[1] Equality in social relations was commonly denied to American blacks. According to Myrdal, it involved an elaborate system of measures to segregate the two groups and prevent them from building up intimate relations (the same phenomenon is found in the case of the Indian caste system). Personal identification of members of the two groups is thereby hindered. Some of these segregation measures have a spatial or institutional character. Others are embodied in an etiquette of racial behaviour.

And being an individualistic society, the segregation between the two races only got intensified.

Ethnic Groups

An ethnic group may be defined as a group of people living in a relationship of complete superordination or subordination with respect to others within a state or economic area.[2] Ethnic groups can be classified not only on the basis of physical attributes but also on the degree of their cultural advancement, the differences in language, religion, nationality and simply by their ways of living. It is only natural that they have to encounter many problems while trying to enter the mainstream. These problems of assimilation are known as 'minority problems'.

Thus, differences among ethnic groups may be a result of variations in culture, such as those claimed by the British, Afrikaan, and Jews of South Africa; or they may rest upon distinguishability, such as those of the whites, East Indians, Bantu, and Cape Coloured of the same area. When the ethnic groups are of the same race—when there are no significant physical characteristics accepted by them as marks of distinction—their process of adjustment involves what are usually termed as 'nationality' or 'minority group' problems. But when they recognise each other physically and use their physical distinction as a basis for the rationale of their interrelationships, their process of adjustment is usually termed 'race relations' or 'race problems'.

Cultural or ethnic groups can be considered as power groups trying to wrest political power from the others. The degree of interethnic conflict can be explained only by the social history of the given relationship. Race and culture are not the true index of the condition of the antagonism. The status as also the circumstances continue to be the same over a long period.

Ethnic relations do not constitute ordered systems but rather antagonistic regimes. On the other hand, political class tends to break up the orderly working of a status system and struggle towards revolutionising it. The aggressive political class aims at social disorder for the purpose of instituting a new order.[3]

The host and the immigrant groups face a great deal of problems when it comes to assimilation and coexistence often with the result that ethnic hatred intensifies. Cox quotes Lloyd Warner on the differences between the host and immigrant cultures.[4] According to him, these systems are peaceful, but while saying so he has not described the background of the system. Secondly, systems of any kind are not always peaceful. Cox describes the relation between the power groups, but not the relation between weak and strong power groups like the blacks and the whites (in the Indian situation, the Brahmins and the dalits). The ethnic groups leading a life distinct from that in the mainland but in close proximity with nature are not assimilated quickly. On the contrary, ethnic antagonism may so suffuse other interests that political class differences are constantly held in abeyance.[5]

Definition of Race

It is evident that the term 'race relations' may include all situations of contact between people of different races, for all time. There is no universally accepted definition of race. Biologists, anthropologists and sociologists differ considerably over the definition of race. For the sociologist, the meanings and definitions a society gives to certain social phenomena and situations are most interesting. For example, an Indian in the US (of white complexion) is not treated as white. For the whites in the US blacks and Indians are the same and both are treated as blacks.

According to Cox, we may think of race relations, therefore, as that behaviour which develops among people who are aware of each other's actual or perceived physical differences. Moreover, by race relations we do not mean all social contact between persons of different 'races', but only those contacts which are determined by a consciousness of a 'racial' difference. If, for example, two persons of different racial strains were to meet and deal with each other on their own devices—that is to say, without being preoccupied with a social definition of each other's race—then it might be said that race here is of no sociological significance. But if their behaviour tended to be fashioned by ethnic attitudes toward each other's actual or perceived physical differences, then the situation may be called a social contact between ethnics, and it may be also referred to as race relations.

The ethnic attitudes are, however, based upon other and more fundamental social phenomena. There is the 'we' feeling as against the 'others'. This attitude seems to be a function of group solidarity, which is not necessarily a racial phenomenon.

Neither is social intolerance.[6] But one can raise the question as to why there should be group solidarity and for whom.

Genesis of Racial Antagonism

There is racial antagonism or social displeasure or resentment against a group which refuses to conform to the established practices and beliefs of the society. The term 'racism', as it has been recently employed in literature, seems to refer to a philosophy of racial antipathy. Studies on the origin of racism involve the study of the development of an ideology, an approach which usually results in the narration of the history, and even rationalising, of a social fact.

Racism is the phenomenon of exploitation of people in a capitalistic society. Again, one would miss the point entirely if one were to think of racial antagonism as having its genesis in some 'social instinct' of antipathy between people.[7]

The phenomenon of racial antagonism had its rise only in modern times: racial exploitation and racial prejudice developed among the Europeans with the rise of capitalism and nationalism. All racial antagonisms can be traced to the policies and attitudes of the capitalists, of Europe and North America.[8]

Identifying capitalism as the cause for racial discrimination, however, may not be the right approach. If the blacks were slaves due to capitalism then why were the whites not enslaved. Why is it that the masters were always the whites and the slaves were all blacks?

Gunnar Myrdal argues that the enslavement of the Negro acquired biological justification only at a later stage. He writes:

> When the Negro was first enslaved, his subjugation was not justified in terms of his biological inferiority. Prior to the influences of the Enlightenment, human servitude was taken as a much more unquestioned element in the existing order of economic class and social estates, since this way of thinking was taken over from feudal and post-feudal Europe. The

> historical literature in this early period also records that the imported Negroes—and the captured Indians—originally were kept in much the same status as the white indentured servants;[9] later the Negroes gradually were pushed down into chattel slavery while the white servants were allowed to work off their bond. The need was felt for some kind of justification beyond the theory of economic expediency and the might of the strong.
>
> The arguments based on this thesis easily merged into the dogma of natural inequality. The arguments were broadly these: that the Negro was a heathen and barbarian, an outcast among the peoples of the earth, a descendant of Noah's son Ham, cursed by God himself and doomed to be a servant, forever, on account of an ancient sin.[10]

Myrdal's approach is misleading where the attempt is to gain a proper understanding of the history of exploitation.

Cox gives a historical description of race relations which is discussed below.

Historical View of Race Relations

In the Middle Ages, there was no instance of racial antagonism in Europe; in fact, Europeans were, at this time, more isolated and ignorant about foreign people and world geography than the Greeks. But, gradually, under a commercial and religious impulse, Europe began to awaken to journey towards strange lands. The First Crusade may be taken as the starting point which finally led to world dominance by Europeans. The discovery of America and the circumnavigation of the globe were the two most important factors which led the Europeans to colonise far-flung lands and develop the means to deal with non-Christian people.

After the eleventh century, the Crusades by the European nations were sanctioned by the Church. The traders followed the clergy and the process of conquering new lands was completed and reinforced by economic exploitation of non-Europeans.

In fact, it was this need for trade with the East, especially by the Italian, Spanish, and Portuguese merchants, and its obstruction by the Mohammedans which began the great drama that was, in a few hundred years, to turn over the destiny of the world to the decisions of businessmen. But our concern at this point is to indicate that racial antagonism had not yet developed among the Europeans.

In the first place, the geography of the world was still a mystery, and some of the most fantastic tales about the foreign peoples were believed. Stories of the splendour, luxury and wisdom of the peoples of the East held all Europe in constant wonderment. The white man then had no conception of himself as a being capable of developing the superior culture of the world—the concept 'white man' had not yet achieved its significant social definition; the Anglo-Saxon, the modern master race, was then not even in the picture.

Even when the Portuguese, moving down the African coast, encountered the Moors and heathens whom they considered inferior to themselves both as fighters and as culture builders, they formed no conclusions about racial superiority. Henry the Navigator, himself, sought in those parts a Christian prince, Prester John, with whom he planned to form an alliance "against the enemies of the faith". All through the latter half of the fifteenth century the Portuguese sailors and explorers kept up this search for the kingdom of the lost black prince.

There was as yet no belief in any cultural incapacity of these coloured peoples. Their conversion to Christianity was sought with enthusiasm, and this transformation was supposed to make the Africans the human equals of all other Christians. The Portuguese historian, Gomes Eannes de Azurara, writing in the middle of the fifteenth century, gives us some idea of the religious motives for Prince Henry's exploits among the peoples on the West African coast. According to him, one reason for Henry the Navigator's slave raids,

> was his great desire to make increase in the faith of our lord Jesus Christ and to bring to him all souls that should be saved—understanding that all the mystery of the Incarnation, Death, and Passion of our Lord Jesus Christ was for this sole end, namely the salvation of lost souls.

An understanding of this matter of cultural conversion is crucial. For the full profitable exploitation of a people, the dominant group must devise ways and means of limiting that people's cultural assimilation. So long as the Portuguese and Spaniards continued to accept the religious definition of human equality, so long also the development of race prejudice was inhibited. The early days of the conquests, especially by the Portuguese and the Spaniards, were not rationalised with the philosophy of racial superiority. To kill or to take into slavery the heathen or infidel was to serve the highest purpose of God. It was the crusading spirit that reigned supreme in them; the economic basis of racial antagonism and rationalisation of inborn inferiority were yet to develop in them. The obsession with the spiritual values of conversion left the Negroes free to be integrated into the general population.

The next era in the history of race relations commenced with the discovery of America. When we consider race prejudice to be an attitudinal instrument of modern human economic exploitation, it becomes clear that racial prejudice was not found among the primitive peoples of the world. Nor did the early explorers of America have any feelings of instinctive hatred towards the natives.[11] When the invaders lost interest with the East, the bourgeois world began to dominate the proceedings. The socio-economic matrix of racial antagonism involved the commercialisation of human labour in the West Indies, the East Indies, and in America, the intense competition among businessmen of different western European cities for the capitalist exploitation of the resources of this area, the development of nationalism and the consolidation of European nations, and the decline of the influence of the Roman Catholic Church with its mystical inhibitions to the free exploitation of economic resources. Racial antagonism attained full maturity during the latter half of the nineteenth century and the great nationalistic powers of Europe began to justify their economic designs upon weaker peoples with subtle theories of racial superiority and masterhood. Western scholars were desperately looking for some theory to explain their military, economic and cultural accomplishments. Probably, the most widely accepted theory was the Biblical story of the descendants of Ham as a people cursed forever to do the menial work of others.

If we had to point out the year which marked the beginning of modern race relations we should select the year 1493–94. This was the time when there was a total disregard for the human rights and physical power of the non-Christian peoples of the world, the coloured peoples, was officially assumed by the first two great colonising European nations. The Treaty of Tordesillas (7 June, 1494), arrived at through diplomatic negotiations between Spain and Portugal, put all the coloured peoples of the world at the mercy of Spain and Portugal.[12]

Sometimes, it is not realised that the slave trade was simply a way of recruiting labour for the purpose of exploiting the great natural resources of America.[13] This trade did not develop because Indians and Negroes were red and black, or because they had inferior mental capacities but simply because they were the best workers to be found for the heavy labour in the mines and plantations across the Atlantic.[14] If white workers were available in sufficient numbers they would have been substituted. As a matter of fact, part of the early demand for labour in the West Indies and on the mainland was filled by white servants, who were sometimes defined in exactly the same terms as the Africans. Although the recruitment of involuntary labour finally settled down to the African coasts, the early kidnappers did a brisk business in some of the most enlightened European cities. Moreover, in the process of exploiting the natural resources of the West Indies, the Spanish invaders literally consumed the native Indian population.

This, then, is the beginning of modern race relations. It was not an abstract, natural, immemorial feeling of mutual antipathy between groups, but rather a practical exploitative relationship with its socio-attitudinal facilitation—at that time, only nascent race prejudice. This peculiar kind of exploitation developed and took a definite capitalistic form with the white man repeating the process round the world among practically every people of colour. Earl Grey was correct when he described, in 1880, the motives and purpose of the British in one racial situation:

> Throughout this part of the British Dominions the coloured people are generally looked upon by the whites as an inferior race, whose interest ought to be systematically disregarded when they come into competition with their own, and who ought to be governed mainly with a view of the advantage of the superior race. And for this advantage two things are considered to be especially necessary: first, that facilities should be afforded to the white colonists for obtaining possession of land heretofore occupied by the native tribes; and secondly, that the Indian population should be made to furnish as large and as cheap a supply of labour as possible.[15]

But the fact of crucial significance is that racial exploitation is merely one aspect of the problem of the proletarianisation of labour, regardless of the colour of the labourer. Hence, racial antagonism is essentially political-class conflict. The capitalist exploiter, being opportunistic and practical, will utilise any convenience to keep his labour and other resources freely exploitable. He will devise and employ race prejudice when that becomes convenient.[16] As a matter of fact, the white proletariat of early capitalism had to endure burdens of exploitation quite similar to those which many coloured peoples had to bear later.

As the capitalist profit-making motive was constantly inhibited by the philosophy and purpose of the Roman Catholic Church, the need was for an ideology, a social theory supporting the capitalist drive for the impersonal exploitation of the workers justifying involuntary servitude. The need was urgent as the destructive consequences of the ruthless enslavement of the Indians was opposed on religious grounds by persons such as the celebrated priest, Las Casas in the West Indies. "The Indians were represented as lazy, filthy pagans, of bestial morals, no better than dogs, and fit only for slavery, in which state alone there might be some hope of instructing and converting them to Christianity."[17] The capitalist exploitation of the coloured workers, it should be observed, consigned them to employment and treatment that was humanly degrading. In order to justify this treatment the exploiters must argue that the workers are innately degraded and degenerate, and consequently, they naturally merit their condition.

In 1550, finally, the great capitalist interests produced a champion, Gaines de Sepulveda, brilliant theologian and debater, to confront Las Casas in an open debate at Valladolid on the right of Spaniards to wage wars of conquest against the Indians. Sepulveda contrived a reasonably logical justification for the irrepressibly exploitative situation. As a characteristic, it should be observed that no explanation at all need have been given to the exploited people themselves. The group sentiment and feeling of the exploited people were disregarded entirely.

Sepulveda, then, may be thought of as among the first great racists.[18] His argument was, in effect, that the Indians were inferior to the Spaniards, therefore they should be exploited. Yet, the powerful religious interest among the Spaniards limited the establishment of a clear philosophy of racial exploitation. Some years earlier, an attempt had been made to show that the Indians were incapable of conversion[19] but this was finally squelched. It remained for later thinkers, mainly from northern European countries, to produce evidence that 'native peoples' had an inferior, animal-like capacity for culture.[20] They were incapable of cultural conversion and their incapacity stood as a bar to movements for cultural assimilation of such people.

The ultimate purpose of all theories of white superiority is not a demonstration that whites are in fact superior to all other human beings but rather to insist that whites must be supreme. And, the world position of a race tends, moreover, to determine the attitude of its members in their relationship with other races. Thus, the English in India derived their dominant attitude not only from the might of the nation which they represented but also from the position which white people occupied over the whole world. "The British were, in fact, a ruling race," to quote Cox.[21]

The whites distinguished themselves by their colour and dominated the other races and castes as well. This type of racial antagonism divides the society vertically. This superiority complex also produces power relationships. Race problems, then, are social problems which have reference to groups physically identifiable. Therefore, we should expect two races in contact and having some basic racial antagonism to develop different problems for persons with different degrees of admixture. And such is, in fact, the case. For instance, in the United States, an African-American resembling the Negro is confronted with different problems from both the white and black person. Ordinarily, the disinterested public treats this white Negro like a white man and insists that he behave like one. Thus, he may be forcibly prevented from sitting among blacks in public conveyances. Similarly a dark complexioned Negro may be assaulted on the highway because his Negro wife resembles a white person. So also if a man with African ancestry, say a Puerto Rican, goes to a barber shop in Honolulu which seeks to attract tourist patronage, he can get his hair cut. But if a man with African blood, identifying himself as a Negro of mainland origin, seeks the service of this shop he is told that he has come to the wrong place.

Slavery

In some cultures, slavery is normal, in others, there is extreme class subordination, and in still others outcasting defiant members is a common practice.

The condition of slavery was probably the purest form of established race relations. Without disguise it defined the slaves, the coloured people, as chattel, and exploited them in production virtually on the same economic principle as that employed in the exploitation of the beasts of burden. It is in this situation that the capitalist, exploitative basis of race relations with its powerful drive towards dehumanising the worker was most clearly observed. The master may consciously decide to use up his slaves because their replacement is cheaper than their conservation.

The coloured people did not have social status in the sense that whites enjoyed. The slave derived his social status not particularly from any attribute of his own, but from the social status and power of his master. In other words, a slave who had ingratiated himself with a powerful master was likely to be treated with circumspection by whites of the community. An ill-treatment of such a slave would be construed as disrespect towards the master. On the whole, however, slaves were not respected as individuals; among the slaves themselves there was no self-respect independent of the master. Indeed, the slave could have no personality capable of responsible, self-assertive behaviour. His individuality remained submerged beneath the overwhelming authority of the master.

The sexual and familial life of the slaves were determined by the master. Slaves could be bred and raised like animal stock, with one or a few males functioning as masters to a community of breeding females. Children, of course, were the property of the masters who were known to marry slave women. This relationship, however, had been usually forbidden by law; concubinage was somewhat more common.

Ordinarily, the sexual relations between master and slave were promiscuous and, in the southern states of the United States at any rate, even this never gained social sanction. In fact, the primary social definition of the slave as a subsocial, working animal led to the corollary definition of sex relations between white men and slave women as sodomy; the white man "defiled his body by lying with a Negro". Quite frequently, however, the powerful sexual urge confronted by the easy sexual opportunities overrode social fiction and many mulatto children were born. The latter, in turn, became socially restless and consequently, more or less, serious threats to the system.

In such a situation, sex relations between slave men and white women were very rare. Marriage, of course, could not be sanctioned; the social disadvantages to the white woman of even a clandestine relationship were so great that she was effectively inhibited. A pregnancy of this kind was a social calamity of the first order. To bear such a child was to 'dishonour God' and abuse one's self most shamefully. A white woman knew that then she would be scorned and ridiculed as a sexual pervert by her community; her coloured child would also present her with an insoluble social problem.

Since the coloured man, the slave, was as good as a social non-entity, slave women who had become concubines of white men gained in social status. Such women rose in the estimation of other slaves and were even envied by interested white women. The relationship, however, was always more or less surreptitious. It was probably most convenient among great plantation owners who practically dominated the community.

Slavery determined the behaviour pattern of the slaves. The purposeful, independent slave was ordinarily 'sold down the river'; the runaway or insurrectionist, 'the lover of freedom', was ordinarily 'broken on the wheel' or 'quartered'. The obsequious, ingratiating and resigned slave ordinarily reached the best adjustment in the system. The Bush Negroes of the Guiana, the Maroons of Jamaica, and the runaways in the northern United States are examples of slaves breaking away to freedom, yet slaves as a whole achieved some workable degree of accommodation.

The finally accommodated slave, a rather exceptional individual in modern slavery, conceived of himself as inconsequential and worthless until he was able to satisfy his master by his work; he also would define the members of his group as having no other reason for existence. This supine devotion of the accommodated slave and the tremendous power of the master over his life and fate could occasionally affect the master so deeply that in sympathy the relationship became personalised and much of the cruel necessities of exploitation were tempered with condescension. Matthew G. Lewis, an absentee Jamaican planter, presents, in his *Journal of a West Indian Proprietor*, a classic illustration of accommodated slaves:

> Whether the pleasure of the Negroes was sincere may be doubted; but certainly it was the loudest that I ever witnessed: they all talked together, sang, danced, shouted, and, in the violence of their gesticulations, tumbled over each other, and rolled upon the ground....
>
> The shouts, the gaiety, the wild laughter, their strange and sudden bursts of singing and dancing, and several old women, wrapped up in large cloaks, their heads bound round with different-coloured handkerchiefs, leaning on a staff, and standing motionless in the middle of the hubbub.

Struggle of the 'social conscience' with itself has characterised the mental state of whites throughout their history of dominance over Negroes. The following rationalisation by the Reverend J.C. Postell of South Carolina in 1836 is not only typical of the period but also illustrates a necessary striving to synchronise beliefs and practices:

> It [slavery] is not a moral evil. The fact that slavery is of Divine appointment, would be proof enough with the Christians that it could not be a moral evil. If slavery was either the invention of man or a moral evil, it is logical to conclude that the power to create has the power to destroy. Why then has it existed? And why does it now exist amidst all the power of legislation in State and Church, and the clamour of the abolitionists? It is the Lord's doings and marvellous in our eyes; and had it not been for the best, God alone, who is able, long since would have overruled it.[22]

Black-White Relations in the USA

As American century comes to a close, we are losing our ability to say what it means to be an American. We are forgetting the handful of compelling ideas that have forged individuals from so many backgrounds into one nation, indivisible. We are Italian, American, Chinese-American, African-American, Scots-Irish-American. There are so many hyphenated versions of us we can hardly keep count. We cherish our regional accents, research our family roots, and burst with pride at ethnic dinners. We are proud of where we have arrived from, and rightly so, but we are forgetting that we have always been producer of where we have arrived; producer of saying, "We are all Americans".

The latest symptom of the divisive tendency is President Clinton's Commission on Race. It issued its final report, the culmination of 14 months of 'dialogue' involving 17,000 Americans in 39 states, which signed that America suffers from too little race consciousness. And its recommended remedy? More race consciousness. Before issuing his report, Commission Chairman John Hope Franklin wrote to the President: "The idea that we should aspire to a colour-blind society is an impediment to reducing racial stereotyping.... The best way to reduce racial stereotyping is to be conscious of racial differences." The report recommends that the President make this all-race-all-the-time approach to national unity permanent by institutionalising his Commission on Race. The proposed 'President's Council for One America' would pick up where the commission left off, carrying on the "great and unprecedented conversation about race".

This is the wrong conversation. As I understand where the President is coming from, considering where he grew up, and where John Hope Franklin grew up, and where I grew up. No southerner who has experienced the indignity of black Americans being pushed to the back of the bus, sent to separate hospitals, relegated to separate bathrooms, and kept out of many of the best schools and colleges because of their race can remain indifferent to the legacy of discrimination. And no one can look at our elite college campuses today, at the boardrooms of Fortune 500 companies, and at those who seem permanently consigned to lower paying jobs, without wanting to open opportunity to Americans of all races.

But the President has started the wrong conversation. With all due respect, he has the wrong ideas about what it means to be an American. In his 1997 State of the Union Address, the President said America's greatest strength is its diversity. He must have been the first President of the United States ever to say that, and I hope he will be the last.

Of course, diversity can be a great strength. But diversity is not America's greatest strength. Bosnia is diverse. Rwanda is diverse. Quebec is diverse. Racial and ethnic differences are tearing those places apart. America's greatest strength is that we are the only nation that, as Margaret Thatcher observed, "has so successfully combined people of so many different races and nations within a single culture".

So, should our national conversation be about what pulls us apart? Think about the times when America has been at her best: winning our freedom at Lexington and Concord, defending that freedom on the beaches of Normandy, and marching together in Selma, Alabama, to secure freedoms for every American. During those times we united around a common set of principles: equal opportunity, individual rights, self-government. From these principles flows the path to racial reconciliation.

Though the framing of the American Constitution in 1787 put slavery in the spotlight—how could it fit in a new society committed to democratic ideals, slavery thrived in the USA with the rise of the cotton industry in the southern states. It was only after slavery was abolished in the British Empire that the British abolitionists turned their attention to the USA. In course of time, American anti-slavery became a crusade. Thomas Jefferson (1743–1826), the third president of the USA, himself made several attacks on the institution of slavery. He wrote in his autobiography:

> It was found that the public mind would not bear the proposition (of gradual emancipation), nor will it bear it even to this day. Yet, the day is not far when it must bear it, or the worse will follow. Nothing is more certainly written in the book of fate than the fact that these people are to be free.

But though Jefferson and his contemporaries emphasised equality of rights to the weaker, there was a fundamental divide in the south. The fight against slavery was seen as an attack on the southern way of life itself. As explained by Cox, the entry of white merchants in the south was the first attack on blacks not only physically but also culturally. Next, they became the ruling class and the blacks were uprooted.

In attempting to understand the motivation of segregation and discrimination, one basic fact must be taken into account, that is, of course, that many blacks, particularly in the south, have been poor, uneducated, and deficient in health but this is only half of the truth about the blacks.

William Archer, who was among the early English observers of the racial problem in America and who, probably better than anyone else, was able to withstand the influence of race prejudice, called for separation in railroad travelling for this reason: "It is the crowding, the swamping, the submerging of the white race by the black, that the south can't reasonably be expected to endure."[23]

This issue is, however, much more complicated. There were a class of southern white men who were also poor, uneducated, coarse and dirty. But there was fundamental equality among all white people, which was the explicit assumption of the slavery doctrine, and, on the other hand, a great gulf between the whites and the blacks. As Embree points out: "The attitude of the aristocrat and of the poor white, starting from arguing opposite motives, often result in the same discrimination."[24]

The basic ideological problem of whites in their relationship with blacks, then, is that of reconciling two standards of morality. The powerful democratic Christian beliefs developed in western society are on the side of the black; the racially articulate whites are for demonstrating that these beliefs do not include coloured people.[25]

There have been cases of Indians (particularly from Punjab) in the United States, who had long since given up the turban and the beard as soon as they understood the nature of black-white relationship, returned to the Oriental dress—a feature that distances them from the Americans. As Hindus, they were conceded certain privileges and opportunities which were denied to blacks of even much lighter complexion. But not so in the South African province of Natal. In the United States, the Hindu is still a romantic figure; in South Africa he is a 'damn coolie'.

It is a fact that a large class of whites have been economically better off than the masses constituting the blacks. The white man identifies himself with 'the white race' and feels that he has a stake in resisting the dissipation of his racial identity of "the absolute and unchangeable superiority of the white race".[26]

It is found that social restrictions on inter-marriage focus on white women. For them it covers both formal marriage and illicit intercourse. With regard to men it is taken more or less for granted that they would not stoop to marry black women, and also that, illicit intercourse does not fall under the same intense taboo. Their maternity is more certain than paternity, and the white race easily avoids intimate relationship with African-Americans as they consider it as pollution. It means that in the US, every single measure is defended as necessary to black 'social equality' which in its turn is held necessary to prevent 'inter-marriage'.

Gunnar Myrdal[27] is of the view that since all mixed blood are classified as Negroes, sex relations between white men and coloured women affect only the Negro race and not the white race. From the white person's point of view it is not 'amalgamation' in the crucial sense. From the same point of view the race of the father does not matter for the racial classification of a black child. The child is a Negro anyhow. Sex relations between black men and white women, on the other hand, would be like an attempt to assimilate African-American blood into the white race. This does not succeed as the child is considered an African-American. But the white woman would be absolutely degraded; white man in the parallel situation is not.

Generally speaking, many believe that co-operation and goodwill between white and coloured races will surely come if the whites are assured that the coloured race has given up all design upon race mixture.[28]

Inter-marriage, however, is a way to end all problems of race relations. In racially dichotomised societies the status quo cannot be maintained without drastic sanctions against white woman-coloured man marriage. In other words, the white woman is here in a critical position; defending her 'purity' becomes a sacred duty. We may assume that the race problem is solved when the white woman becomes free to follow her sentiments in choosing either white man or coloured man in marriage.

Lamar Alexander, in his article "Created Equal", is of the view that while America as a nation reflects unity in diversity, the emphasis should be on 'unity' and not its 'diversity'. Here, he refers to President Clinton's Commission on Race and criticises its suggestion for greater race consciousness. He opines that diversity is not America's greatest strength as President Clinton had emphasised. Rather, America's strength lies in combining different races and nations into a single culture (see Annexure 1).

White Liberalism

Shelby Steele, focusing on the trend of white liberalism in the United States in the post-1960s era, discusses a basic flaw in it: firstly, its emphasis on national redemption rather than the actual issue of self-sufficiency and equality for blacks, and secondly, confusing the white mandate for redemption with interventions like affirmative action resulting in group preferences and entitlements for the blacks and not actual efforts to end black discrimination and promote black development. Thus, racial reform in the country is a hollow concept lacking integrity: it comforts the white conscience and makes happy the black grievance for which preferences mean patronage to insure its own power. It does not effect reform according to democratic principles and with a view to help blacks achieve parity (see Annexure 2).

The modern trend of white liberalism discussed above, preoccupied with interventions through affirmative action, can be viewed as the outcome of significant developments in the blacks' struggle for civil rights in the 1960s. Increasing pressure led to the passage of federal legislation, the Civil Rights Acts of

1964 and 1968, and the Voting Rights Act of 1965 which made a guarantee of equal rights under the law and prohibition of discrimination in schools, employment, public facilities and voting. The most prominent figure in the civil rights movement at this time was Martin Luther King, who led the landmark Montgomery bus boycott in Alabama in 1955, which catapulted him to fame, and was prominent in organising the historic march of 2,00,000 people from all over the USA in Washington DC in 1963 to demand racial equality.

Notes

1. Myrdal, Gunnar, *An American Dilemma*, Harper & Row Publishers, New York, 1944, p. 573.
2. Cox, Oliver C., *Caste, Class and Race*, Modern Reader Paperbacks, New York, 1948.
3. Abraham Lincoln was pertinent when in 1848 he said in Congress: "It is a quality of revolution not to go by old lines and old laws; but to break up both, and make new ones." Nicolay, J.G. and Hay, John, *Abraham Lincoln: Complete Works*, Vol. I, p. 105.
4. It appears that the principle of racial and nationality assimilation laid down by Lloyd Warner and Leo Srole is too simple. As they see it,

   > The greater the difference between the host and the immigrant cultures, the greater will be the subordination, the greater the strength of ethnic social systems, and the longer the period necessary for assimilation of the ethnic groups ... The greater the racial difference the greater ... the subordination of the immigrant group... and the longer the period necessary for assimilation.

   The process of assimilation is further delayed if the immigrant is divergent in both cultural and physical traits. There is probably some truth in this birds-of-a-feather hypothesis, yet it seems that it may be too truistic and crude for significant analysis of internationality and racial assimilation. See *The Social Systems of American Ethnic Groups*, pp. 285–86.

5. Edgar H. Brookes describes the situation in South Africa which illustrates this:

   Economically the Poor White, the Coloured man and the detribalised, urban Native are in the same category. Yet no political party in South Africa, with the exception of the Communists, has made any serious or sustained attempt to draw them all together in opposition to capitalism. It is most significant that the poor white proletariat of the towns does not in general vote for Communist or even for Labour candidates but for some party—whether the main National Party or not—which claims to be 'nationalist'. They are not class-conscious. They prefer to join with their fellow-workers... As was long the case in the Southern States of America, as indeed still is the case there, the Poor White has sacrificed his economic to his sentimental interests, and the immediate economic protection offered him on colour lines (*The Colour Problems of South Africa*, p. 29).

6. See Arendt, Hannah, "Race-Thinking Before Racism", *The Review of Politics*, Vol. 6, January 1944, pp. 36–73; and Detwelier, Fredrick G. "The Rise of Modern Race Antagonism", *The American Journal of Sociology*, Vol. 37, March 1932, pp. 738–47.
7. Consider, for instance, the following definitive statement by Professor Robert E. Park:

   This prejudice against the Japanese is due to the existence in the human mind of a mechanism by which we inevitably and automatically classify every individual human being we meet. When a race bears an external mark by which every individual member of it can infallibly be identified, that race is by that fact set apart and segregated. Japanese, Chinese and Negroes can not move among us with the same freedom as members of other races because they bear marks which identify them as members of their race. This fact isolates them... Isolation is at once a cause and an effect of race prejudice. It is a vicious circle—isolation, prejudice; prejudice, isolation (in Steiner, Jesse F., *The Japanese Invasion*, p. xvi).

Since, however, we may assume that all races "bear marks which identify them as members of their race," it must follow, according to Park, that a certain human capacity for classification makes it impossible for races to come together without racial antagonism and prejudice. But this instinct-emphasising hypothesis is too simple.

8. Cf. Brown, Ina Corine, *National Survey of the Higher Education of Negroes,* U.S. Office of Education, Misc. No. 6, Vol. I, pp. 4–8. Professor G.A. Bogese makes an observation pertinent to this remark:

   The English-speaking mind is not fully alive to the gravity of this issue. Unlike their German cousins and foes, the Anglo-Saxon stocks did not strive to become the master race of *Herrenvolk* holding sway over the world and mankind... Yet, unlike their German cousins and rivals, they have succeeded in being a *Herrenvolk,* a race of masters (italics Bogese's). "Europe Wants Freedom from Shame", *Life,* March 12, 1945, pp. 41–42.

   The Germans needed all of Hitler's ranting and daily doses from the Goebbels propaganda machine to persuade them that they were better than other people. Englishmen simply take it for granted and rarely waste a syllable discussing it. See Scott, John, *Europe in Revolution,* p. 216.

9. See, for example: Russell, John H., *The Free Negro in Virginia, 1619–1865* (1913); Ballagh, J.C., *A History of Slavery in Virginia* (1902); Hurd, John C, *The Law of Freedom and Bondage in the United States (1858–1862).*

10. A weak variation of this popular theory—weak because it looked forward only to temporary subordination of backward peoples—was that by making the blacks slaves white men were educating and christianising them. This variation is known as the 'white man's burden' doctrine and played an especially important role in the nineteenth century exploitation. For more views on this doctrine, see Browen W.Q., "Rationalisation of Race Prejudice", *The International Journal of Ethics* (April, 1933), pp. 299–301.

11. Although Columbus participated in the enslavement of the Indians of the West Indies, which finally led to their extermination, his first impression of them is well known:

They are a loving uncovetous people, so docile in all things that I do assure your Highness I believe in all the world there is not a better people or better country; they love their neighbours as themselves, and they have the sweetest and gentlest way of speaking in the world and always with a smile...

As they showed us such friendship and as I recognised they were people who would yield themselves better to the Christian faith and be converted more through love than by force, I gave them some coloured buttons and some glass beads ... and (they) became so attached to us that it was a marvel to behold.

See MacNutt, Francis A., *Bartholomew De Las Casas*, pp. 18, 19.

12. As early as 1455, Pope Nicholas V had granted the Portuguese exclusive right to their discoveries on the African coast, but the commercial purpose here was still very much involved with the crusading spirit.
13. In a discussion of the arguments over slavery during the Constitutional Convention, Charles A. Beard observes:

    South Carolina was particularly determined, and gave northern representatives to understand that if they wished to secure their commercial privileges, they must make concessions to the slave trade. And they were met halfway. Ellsworth said: "As slaves multiply so fast in Virginia and Maryland that it is cheaper to raise than import them, whilst in the sickly rice swamps foreign supplies are necessary, if we go no farther than is urged, we shall be unjust towards South Carolina and Georgia. Let us not intermeddle. As population increases, poor labourers will be so plenty as to render slaves useless" (*An Economic Interpretation of the Constitution,* p. 177. Quote from Farrand, Max, Records, Vol. II, p. 371).

14. In a discussion of the labour situation among the early Spanish colonists in America, Professor Bailey W. Diffie observes: "One Negro was reckoned as worth two, four, or even more Indians at work production," *Latin American Civilisation*, p. 206.

15. Quoted by Morel, E.D., *The Black Man's Burden*, p. 30.
16. Here, we may tend to give the impression that race prejudice was always manufactured in full awareness by individuals or groups of entrepreneurs. This, however, is not quite the case. Race prejudice, from its inception, became part of the social heritage, and as such both exploiters and exploited for the most part are born heirs to it. Those who propagate and defend race prejudice may not be conscious of its fundamental motivation. To paraphrase Adam Smith: "They who teach and finance race prejudice are by no means such fools as the majority of those who believe and practice it."
17. MacNutt, Francis Augustus, op. cit., p. 83. It should be kept clearly in view that this colonial movement was not a transference of the feudal manorial economy to America. It was the beginning of an entirely different economic enterprise—the dawn of colonial capitalism, the moving out of 'white' capital into the lands of coloured peoples who had to be exploited unsentimentally and with any degree of ruthlessness in the interest of profits (Mac Nutt, op. cit., p. 288).
18. Among the Spanish writers of the time (about 1535 onward) who were in rather complete accord with the drastic methods of human exploitation in the New World was Gonzolo Fernandez de Oviedo, whose prolific works have been collected in the commentary, *Historia Generally Natural de las Indias* (four vols). It was Oviedo's opinion, even after visiting America on a royal commission, that the Indians were not far removed from the state of wild animals and that coercive measures were necessary if they were to be Christianised and taught the uses of systematic labour.
19. MacNutt, op. cit., pp. 94–95.
20. Oliver C. Cox notes that beasts of burden do not have rights which human beings are bound to respect; they may be exploited at will. The latter convenience is a desideratum in the capitalist exploitation of labour, regardless of the colour of the labourer. However, the fact of difference in colour and culture makes available to the exploiters of coloured workers a valuable means of securing their dehumanisation in the eyes of a certain public, that is to say, the public of the exploiting class. When a philosophy for the dehumanising of the exploited people has been developed with sufficient cogency, the ruling class is ready

to make it a grand statement, sometimes implicitly, and to act in accordance with it: the coloured people have no rights which the master race is bound to respect. The exploiting class has an economic investment in this conviction and it will defend it with the same vigour as it would an attack upon private property in land and capital (Cox, 1948).

21. Cox, p. 427.
22. Parker, Pillsbury, *The Church as it is,* quoted by Bowen, Trevor, *Divine White Right,* p. 107.
23. To continue with Archer's thought:

> But elbow-room is just what the conditions of railway travelling preclude; wherefore I hold the system of cars a legitimate measure of difference against constant discomfort. Had it not been adopted, the South would have been a nation of saints, not of men. It is in the methods of its enforcement that they sometimes show themselves not only human but inhuman (*Through Afro-America,* 1910, p.72).

24. Embree, Edwin R., *Brown America*, 1933, p. 205.
25. To be sure, these beliefs are not in themselves social determinants; they merely evince the basic ideological conflict between two social systems—those of the democratic proletariat and the oligarchic capitalists.
26. Again the prevalent sentiment is best exemplified by a citation of old literature. The rhetorical intensity of the following paragraphs from Henry W. Grady gives something of the emotional tone of even present-day popular view:

> But the supremacy of the white race of the South must be maintained forever, and the domination of the Negro race resisted at all points and at all hazards, because the white race is the superior race. This is the declaration of no new truth; it has abided forever in the marrow of our bones and shall run forever with the blood that feeds Anglo-Saxon hearts (op. cit., p. 104).

27. Myrdal, Gunnar, p. 589.
28. R.F. Alfred, speaking with reference to the South African situation, says:

For the fear of race-mixture, the most we can aim at and hope is to reduce such relations to small proportions, by establishing the firmest possible will in both groups to maintain the rule that white shall marry white and black shall marry black, and that extramarital relations between white and black, with the resulting additions to the coloured population, are ... to be avoided. It is a principle which has been established as one of the defining elements in group pride and group identity of the whites, and it is becoming similarly a defining element in the group pride and group identity of the Bantu. To ask whether it is right or wrong that both groups should build themselves upon this principle seems to me irrelevant and futile... ("Race Mixture and Native Policy in South Africa" in Shapera, op. cit., pp. 278–79).

2

Caste System in India

It appears that the term caste, used in the Aryan context, refers to different races and the different castes do not have a religion. Defining caste and examining its origin in ancient Indian society, it is interesting to study the various theories by scholars especially the colour-based theories recognising the Aryans' passion to protect their light colour from intermixture. Despite increasing rigidity of the caste system over time, it has been pointed out that there was always some amount of caste mobility owing to economic and political reasons. An important phase in the history of the caste system began with India's colonisation by the European powers particularly the British who not only introduced new terms of discourse on caste but effected changes in the system itself. In India, following independence, the terms and categories for describing the qualitative changes in the caste system came to be derived from the colonial discourse. In independent India, attempts at secularisation of caste have involved deritualisation and politicisation: as a result, the caste system has witnessed a major transformation. Caste has been pushed out of the traditional stratificatory system and linked to the new structure of representational power, for instance.

The caste system in India is social stratification of society broadly into four varnas; the term 'varna' originally meaning 'colour'. In this sense, the existence of various caste groups within a society is a scenario not dissimilar to the prevalence of different racial groups in a society. As noted by scholar M.K. Sharma:

> In all countries, the social groups are called ethnic identities and races. In a small country like Yugoslavia, there are six races and six republics. Then, why call the Indian races as castes, and spread the tomfoolery that the term caste has some other meaning—other than ethnic identity and race?[1]

Dr. Ambedkar clarifies this when he says in a brochure titled "Castes in India", that "we can say that there are three castes in America broadly—the caste of whites, the black caste and the Red Indian caste." This way, the term caste is a generic term and is used synonymously with races. Following this logic it appears that the term caste used in the Aryan context denotes different races.

Dr. Ambedkar is of the view that Aryan castes do not have a religion and their 'Aryadharma' or Brahminism is no religion.

According to the famous Indologist, Sir Monier Williams,[2] the word 'Hindu' has a territorial rather than religious significance. He says it refers to

> that part of the great Aryan race which immigrated from Central Asia, through the mountain passes, into India, settled first in the district near the river Sindhu (now called the Indus).The Persians pronounced this word 'Hind' and named their Aryan brethren 'Hindus'; the Greeks who probably gained their first idea of India from the Persians dropped the hard aspirate and called the Hindus 'Indol'. Further, he observes that although there developed several sects and sub sects, thoughts and isms, the word 'Hindu' is all tolerant, all-comprehensive and all-absorbing.

The word 'Hindu' does not refer to a religion in the ordinary sense of the term. According to B.G. Tilak, acceptance of the *Vedas* with reverence and recognition of the fact that the means of salvation are diverse, are among the distinguishing features of Hindu religion.[3] Further, it has been rightly observed by G.J. Gajendragadkar in *Shastri Yagnapursh Dasfi V. Muldas* (1966) that unlike other religions in the world, the Hindu religion does not claim any one God.[4]

Definition of Caste

Caste in India has been defined by M.N. Srinivas as a hereditary, endogamous, usually localised group having a traditional association with an occupation and a particular position in the local hierarchy of castes. Relations between castes are governed, among other things, by the concepts of pollution and purity and generally, maximum commensality occurs within the caste.

Origin of Caste and Caste Mobility

Where origin of caste is concerned, Oliver C. Cox discusses the theory of Sir Herbert Risley, recognised as the most insistent advocate of the racial theory of caste, who explains caste in terms of race relations. A variation of Risley's theory is proposed by Nripendra Kumar Datt who relies upon the word meaning complexion to show that caste emerged with the Aryans' passion to protect their light colour from intermixture with the dark colour of the Dravidians. Cox argues that the colour-based theories fail to impress for lack of historical data. Also, the contention that the Indo-Aryans had no scruples to inter-marry among themselves—thus, there was a need to preserve the purity of their 'varna'—has little evidence to support it. Often, inter-marriages were denounced and difficult to carry out (see Annexure 3).

The usual way of making the evidently impossible transition from the racial origin of caste to the non-racial caste system as we know it is to employ some such phrase as, with the hardening of caste rule in the course of time, Yet why should caste rules 'harden'? We should expect them to have been relaxed, for as the population became increasingly mixed—so much so that today brahmins are not infrequently darker in complexion than lower-caste persons—the raison d'etre of caste should have vanished. It would be difficult to accept the proposition that the memory that at one time Aryans protected themselves from intermixture was sufficient to perpetuate the caste system with increasing rigidity.

According to O.P. Goyal, the caste system was never too rigid. Even in the early history of India, the caste system though supposed to be very rigid was not a totally immobilised system. Some amount of mobility was always there within the caste system. Caste determines the relative status of one group as against the other. Status has not only ritual but economic as well as political implications. Therefore, there had been constant efforts even in the early history of India towards mobility. Different castes were able to go up in the hierarchy of castes or go down because of economic and political reasons.

Oliver C. Cox states that in 1498 the Portuguese adventurers who landed at Calicut with Vasco da Gama observed that in India, society was organised in a number of endogamous groups with inferior and superior social positions held in perpetuity. They compared this with the social mobility familiar to them in the West and finally called it *casta*. Since then (about the middle of the sixteenth century) numerous writers have made the same observation. A recognition of relative rigidity of social status among different status systems then, is no contribution of modern sociologists.[5]

Dhiru Bhai Sheth traces the earliest details of European accounts of the Indian caste system in Portuguese attempts to identify the features of the caste system and study its working in society. In an interesting discussion, he argues that as a result of the British colonisation of India the caste structure came to be viewed as an inflexible vertical hierarchy of ritual statuses. It gave rise to new features in the understanding and functioning of the age-old caste system, importantly, a perspective that viewed caste in terms of western categories of values like equality and individualism, and western concepts of race and class, evolution of a multiple system of class classifications and involvement of the state in caste matters—like judging the castes' status claims in the ritual hierarchy. The changes have intensified in independent India where the process of secularisation of caste, as through deritualisation and politicisation, has contributed to the development of a new kind of caste stratified system. With deritualisation or loss of rituality, for instance, caste has ceased to be a unit of the ritual-status hierarchy and survives as a kinship-based cultural community (see Annexure 4).

The general tendency among writers influenced by Hindu philosophy like Dhiru Bhai Sheth is to criticise western thinkers and historians while studying the British attitude towards untouchability. They think that the British were solely responsible for changing the condition of untouchables. Knowingly, the British rulers established the idea of caste system in India. In my view the caste system was already prevailing in India. The British did not make caste in the Indian society although they tabulated the caste system when the first census was started in India. In this context, it is relevant to point out much that is typical of what may be called classical Hinduism. The Hinduism of the *Upanishads* and the later cults derives not from the invading Aryans but, strangely enough, from the populations they conquered, the Dasyus. Throughout this decisive period the descendants of the invaders comprised the upper group, while those of the indigenous people, often called 'Dravidian', constituted the lower group.[6] The *Rigveda* itself introduced the idea of immutability of caste by laying stress upon the fact of birth. The "Purusha Sukta" attributes the origin of each caste to a particular organ. Once the theory was formulated that caste was dependent upon birth, it gradually laid its hold upon the ideology and practice in India, and each succeeding period of history saw its influence spreading in society. Caste in ancient India was an institution, for almost all its ingredients are to be found in the *Vedas*. Race, tribe, class, occupation, creed, and ritual are elements which have gone into its making. In the Aryan society, as reflected in the *Rigveda*, there appears to be a contrast between the Aryan who possessed a fair colour and a fine nose and the Dasyu who was dark and had a snub nose.[7]

The practice of untouchability created a sense of superiority, an attitude of apathy and hatred, and indifference towards the untouchables. According to Kshirsagar[8], untouchability is a comprehensive term which includes each and every practice which aims at suppressing or oppressing the so-called untouchable for no reason. In the words of Mahatma Gandhi, "untouchability is a snake with a thousand mouths through each of which it shows its poisonous fangs."[9] Untouchability is observed, not only against an individual or a few individuals, but against a group of individuals classed as untouchable. A group of so-called high caste people observe untouchability against all the supposed lower caste people. Hence, it has been rightly observed by the Elaya Perumal Committee that "untouchability is an attitude on the part of a whole group of people. It is a spirit of social aggression that underlies this attitude."[10]

Origin of Untouchability

The causes of the origin of untouchability may be studied by examining a few theories that have been advanced as explanation of the origin of this phenomenon in society. Kshirsagar discusses four such theories in detail which identify factors such as a fictitious belief in caste purity and taboo, the subjugation of the non-Aryans by the Aryans who then assigned them menial occupations and the existence, in primitive times, of a floating population constituting 'broken tribesman' from defeated tribes (See Annexure 5).

In the history of caste reforms and particularly abolition of untouchability the name that stands out and apart from the rest is that of Dr. Bhim Rao Ambedkar. He was one of the foremost social reformers to awaken the dalits and make them question their status in society and organise them politically into a ruled front in a struggle for improving their lot.

Race and Caste Compared

According to Oliver C. Cox, caste pride is based upon internal group invidiousness while race pride cuts across caste lines and reaches out to a whole people, commanding their loyalty in a body. The question of whether caste discrimination is crueller than racial discrimination is not very relevant though it was a common practice to point out to Indian nationalists that white people were not nearly so inhuman towards lower castes as the upper castes. He is of the view that the caste system has a gradient of increment of superiority and inferiority from the human degradation to the exalted guru "and unless we can conceive of a society's committing suicide, we should not expect Hindus as a whole to revolt against the system". Take the instance of blacks in their relationship with whites. Blacks in America are solicitous about the fate of Negroes all over the world. The feeling arises from a consciousness of identity of interest in opposing white mastery of their race.

Race conflict is directed either against or towards the maintenance of the entire order of the races, i.e., it questions the racial order itself. On the other hand, caste rivalry never brings the caste system into question; its purview of opposition is circumscribed by identified castes. Races, that is to say, are not status-bearing entities in the sense that castes are. For instance, while African-Americans and whites in the US stand towards each other in a relationship of subordination and superordination, a relationship implying suspended conflict—a power relationship in which definite aims and ends of each group are opposed, castes stand towards each other in a relationship of superiority and inferiority, a relationship implying natural socially accepted, peaceful status ordering of the society—a situation of mutual enviousness among little status-bearing groups.

According to the famous Marathi Dalit writer, Gangadhar Pantawane, the black was neither untouchable in the past nor is so in the present. In contrast, the Indian dalit was and is untouchable. Untouchability is the characteristic of Indian life. Bhim Rao Ambedkar discovered a new phrase for this. He said that in India there is the presence of 'touch-me-not'—untouchability that is more cruel than slavery. While comparing them, Dr. Ambedkar said:

> The slave status carried no stigma on the man in the society. He was touchable and even respectable... untouchability is worse than slavery because a slave has personality in the society, while the untouchable has no personality has been made abundantly clear... Untouchability is worse than slavery because it carries no such security as to livelihood as the latter does. No one is responsible for the feeding, housing and clothing of untouchables. From this point of view untouchability is not only worse than slavery but is positively cruel as compared to slavery. The second or rather the third difference between untouchability and slavery was never obligatory, but untouchability is obliged.

To get a true idea of the position of the untouchables under the Hindu social order, it is necessary to study the working of this phenomenon on a Hindu village. Dr. Ambedkar has given the following picture on the nature of the Indian village:

> The Hindu village is a working plant of the Hindu social order. One can see there the Hindu social order in operation in full swing. The average Hindu is always in ecstasy whenever he speaks of the Indian village. He regards it as an ideal form of social organisation to which he believes there is no parallel anywhere in the world. It is claimed to be a special

contribution to the theory of social organisation for which India may well be proud of.

How fanatic the Hindus are in their belief in the Indian village as an ideal piece of social organisation may be seen from the angry speeches made by the Hindu members of the Indian Constituent Assembly in support of the contention that the Indian Constitution should recognise the Indian village as its base of the constitutional pyramid of autonomous administrative units with its own legislature, executive and judiciary. From the point of view of the untouchables, there could not have been a greater calamity. Thankfully, the Constituent Assembly did not adopt it. Nevertheless the Hindus persist in their belief that the Indian village is an ideal form of social organisation. This belief of the Hindus is not ancestral belief, nor does it come from the ancient past. It is borrowed from Sir Charles Metcalfe—a civil servant of the East India Company. Melcalfe, who was a revenue officer, in one of his Revenue Papers described the Indian village in the following terms:[12]

> The village communities are little republics, having nearly everything they want within themselves and almost independent of any foreign relations. They seem to last when nothing else lasts. Dynasty after dynasty tumbles down, revolution succeeds revolution; Hindu, Pathan, Moghul, Maratha, Sikh, English, all are masters in turn, but the village communities remain the same. In times of trouble they arm and fortify themselves. A hostile army passes through the country, the village communities collect their cattle within their walls and let the enemy pass unprovoked. If plunder and devastation be directed against themselves, and the forces employed be irresistible, they flee to friendly villages at a distance; but when the storm has passed over, they return and resume their occupations. If a country remains for a series of years the scene of continued pillage and massacre so that the villages cannot be inhabited, the scattered villagers

> nevertheless return whenever the power of peaceable possession revives. A generation may pass away, but the succeeding generation will return. The sons will take the place of their fathers; the same site for the village, the same position for their houses, the same lands will be reoccupied by the descendants of those who were driven out when the village was repopulated; and it is not a trifling matter that will drive them out, for they will often maintain their post through times of disturbances and convulsion, and acquire strength sufficient to resist pillage and oppression with success. This union of the village communities, each one forming a little state in itself, has, I conceive, contributed more than any other cause to the preservation of the people of India, through all the revolutions and changes which they have referred, and is in a high degree conducive to their happiness and to the enjoyment of a great portion of freedom and independence.

Having read this description of an Indian village given by a high placed member of the governing class, the Hindus felt flattered and adopted his view as a welcome compliment. In adopting this view of the Indian village, the Hindus have not done any justice to their intelligence or their understanding. They have merely exhibited the weakness common to all subject people. Since many foreigners are led to accept this idealistic view of the Indian village, it would be better to present a realistic picture of the society as one finds it in an Indian village.

The Indian village is not a single social unit. It consists of castes. But for our purpose, it is enough to say:

1. The population in the village is divided into two sections: (i) touchables, and (ii) untouchables.
2. The touchables form the major community and the untouchables a minor community.
3. The touchables live inside the village and the untouchables live outside the village in separate quarters.

4. Economically, the touchables form a strong and powerful community, while the untouchables are a poor and a dependent community.
5. Socially, the touchables occupy the position of a ruling race, while the untouchables occupy the position of a subject race of heredity bondsmen.

What are the terms of associated life on which the touchables and untouchables live in an Indian village? In every village the touchables have a code which the untouchables are required to follow. This code lays down the acts of omissions and commissions which the touchables treat as offences. The following is the list of such offences:

1. The untouchables must live in separate quarters away from the habitation of the Hindus. It is an offence for the untouchables to break or evade the rule of segregation.
2. The quarters of the untouchables must be located towards the south, since the south is the most inauspicious of the four directions. A breach of this rule shall be deemed to be an offence.
3. The untouchables must observe the rule of distance pollution or shadow of pollutions as the case may be. It is an offence to break the rule.
4. It is an offence for a member of the untouchable community to acquire wealth, such as land or cattle.
5. It is an offence for a member of the untouchable community to build a house with tiled roof.
6. It is an offence for a member of the untouchable community to put on a clean dress, wear shoes, watches or gold ornaments.
7. It is an offence for a member of the untouchable community to gives high sounding names to his or her children. Their names should be such as to indicate contempt.
8. It is an offence for a member of the untouchable community to sit on a chair in the presence of a Hindu.

9. It is an offence for a member of the untouchable community to ride on a horse or a palanquin through the village.
10. It is an offence for a member of the untouchable community to take a procession of untouchables through the village.
11. It is an offence for a member of the untouchable community not to salute a Hindu.
12. It is an offence for a member of the untouchable community to speak a cultured language.
13. It is an offence for a member of the untouchable community, if he happens to come into the village on a sacred day which the Hindus treat as the day of fast and at or about the time of breaking of fast, to go about speaking, on the grounds that their breath is held to foul the air and the food of the Hindus.
14. It is an offence for an untouchable to wear the outward marks of a touchable and pass himself as a touchable.
15. An untouchable must conform to the status of an inferior and he must wear the marks of his inferiority for the public to know and identify him. These marks are
    (a) having a contemptible name,
    (b) not wearing clean clothes,
    (c) not having tiled roof,
    (d) not wearing silver and gold ornaments.

    A contravention of any of these rules is an offence.

Next come the duties which the code requires members of the untouchable community to perform for the touchables. Under this head the following may be mentioned:

1. A member of an untouchable community must carry a message of any event in the house of a Hindu such as death or marriage to his relatives living in other villages no matter how distant these villages may be.
2. An untouchable must accompany a Hindu when a marriage is taking place, for gathering firewood and going on errands.

3. An untouchable must accompany a Hindu girl when she is going from her parent's house to her husband's village no matter how distant it is.
4. When the whole village community is engaged in celebrating a general festivity such as Holi or Dassara, the untouchables must perform all menial acts which are preliminary to the main observance.
5. On certain festivities, the untouchables must submit their women to members of the village community to be made the subject of indecent fun.

These duties have to be performed without remuneration.

To realise the significance of these duties, it is important to note why they have come into being. Every Hindu in the village regards himself as a superior person above the untouchables. As an overlord, he feels it absolutely essential to maintain his prestige. This prestige he cannot maintain unless he has at his command a retinue to dance attendance on him. It is in the untouchable that he finds a ready retinue which is at his command and for which he does not have to pay. The untouchables by reason of their helplessness cannot refuse to perform these duties and the Hindu villager does not hesitate to exact them since they are so essential to the maintenance of his prestige.

These offences are not to be found in the Penal Code, enacted by the British Government. Nonetheless so far as the untouchables are concerned, they are real. A breach of any of them involves sure punishment for the untouchables. How they are enforced will be made clear in Chapters 5 and 6.

Another important thing to note is that the punishment for these offences is always collective. The whole community of untouchables is liable for punishment though the offence may have been committed by an individual.

How do the untouchables live? How do they earn their living? Without a knowledge of the ways of earning a livelihood which are open to the untouchables it would not be possible to have a clear idea of their place in the Hindu society.

In an agricultural country, agriculture can be the main source of living. But this source of earning a living is generally not open to the untouchables. This is so for a variety of reasons. In the first place purchase of land is beyond their means. Secondly even if an untouchable has the money to purchase land he has no opportunity to do so. In most parts the Hindus would resent an untouchable coming forward to purchase land and thereby trying to become the equal of the touchable class of Hindus. Such an act of daring on the part of an untouchable would not only be frowned upon but might easily invite punishment. In some parts they are disabled by law from purchasing land. For instance in the province of Punjab, there is a law called the Land Alienation Act. This law specifies the communities which can purchase land and the untouchables are excluded from the list. The result is that in most parts the untouchables are forced to be landless labourers. As labourers they cannot demand reasonable wages. They have to work for the Hindu farmer for such wages as their masters choose to give. On this issue the Hindu farmers can get together to keep the wages to the lowest level possible for it is to their interest to do so. On the other hand, the untouchables have no holding power. They must earn or starve. Nor have they any bargaining power. They must submit to the rate fixed or suffer violence.

The wages paid to the untouchables are either paid in cash or in corn. In parts of Uttar Pradesh the corn given to the untouchables as their wages is called 'Gobaraha'. 'Gobaraha' means privy corn or corn contained in the dung of an animal. In the month of March or April when the crop is fully grown, reaped and dried, it is spread on the threshing floor. Bullocks are made to tread over the corn in order to take the corn out of husk by the pressure of their hooves. While treading over the corn, the bullocks swallow up the corn as well as the straw. As their intake is excessive they find it difficult to digest the corn. Next day, the same corn comes out of their stomach along with their dung. The dung is strained and the corn is separated and given to the untouchable workmen as their wages which they convert into flour and make into bread.

When the agricultural season is over the untouchables have no employment and no means of earning a living. In such seasons they subsist by cutting grass and firewood from the jungle and selling it in a nearby town. Even when it is opened it depends upon the forest guard. Only if he is bribed he will let them take some grass and firewood from the government forest. When it is brought to the town they have always to face a buyer's market. The Hindus who are the main body of buyers will always conspire to depress the wages. Having no power to hold out, the untouchables have to sell their stuff for whatever is offered to them. Often they have to walk ten miles each way from the village to the town and back to sell their stuff.

There is no trade in which they are engaged themselves as a means of earning a livelihood. They do not have the capital for it and even if they did, no one would buy from them.

All these sources of earning are obviously precarious and fleeting. There is no security. There is only one secure source of livelihood open to the untouchables in some parts of the country known to me. It is the right to beg food from the Hindu farmers of the village. Every village has its machinery of administration. The untouchables of the village are hereditary menials employed in the village administration. As part of their remuneration the whole body of untouchables get a small parcel of land assigned in the ancient past which is fixed and is never increased and which the untouchables prefer to leave uncultivated because of its excessive fragmentation. Coupled with this is given to them the right to beg for food.

Shocking as it may seem, this has become a customary right of the untouchables and even the government takes into account the value of the food obtained by the untouchables by begging in fixing the remuneration of an untouchable if he were to be employed in a government job.

This right to beg for food from the touchable is now the principal means of livelihood for 60 million untouchables in India. If anyone were to move in a village after the usual dinner time, he will meet with a swarm of untouchables moving about the village begging for food and saluting.

This statutory beggary as a means of livelihood for the untouchables has become a system. The untouchable families are attached to different touchable families in the village as the serfs as villeins were to the lords of the manors in medieval Europe. The untouchable families attached to the touchable families are at the command of the latter. This relationship has become so personal that one always hears a touchable speaking of an untouchable as 'my man' as though he was his slave. This relationship has helped to systematise this manner of begging of food by the untouchables from the touchables' households.

This is the village republic of which the Hindus are so proud. What is the position of the untouchables in this republic? They are not merely the last but are also the least. They are stamped as inferior and are held down to that status by all ways and means which a majority can command. This inferiority is the destiny not merely of an individual but of the whole class. All untouchables are inferior to all touchables irrespective of age or qualification. A touchable youth is above an aged untouchable and an educated untouchable must rank below an illiterate touchable.

The established order is the law made by the touchables. The untouchables have nothing to do with it except to obey it and respect it.

The untouchables have no rights against the touchables. For them there is no equal right, no justice by which that which is due to the untouchables is allowed to them. Nothing is due to them except what the touchables are prepared to grant. The untouchables must not insist on rights. They should pray for mercy and favour and rest content with what is offered.

This established order is a hereditary order both in status as well as in function. Once a touchable, always a touchable. Once an untouchable, always an untouchable. Once a Brahmin, always a Brahmin. Once a sweeper, always a sweeper. Under it, those who are born high, remain high; those who are born low, remain low. In other words, the established order is based on an inexorable law of *karma* or destiny which is fixed once and for all and can never be changed. This destiny has no relation to the merits of the individuals living under it. An untouchable however superior he may be mentally and morally, is below a touchable in rank, no matter how inferior he may be mentally or morally. A touchable however poor he may be, must always take rank above an untouchable, however rich he may be.

Such is the picture of the inside life of an Indian village. In this republic, there is no place for democracy. There is no room for equality. There is no room for liberty and there is no room for fraternity. The Indian village is the very negation of a republic. If it is a republic, it is a republic of the touchables, by the touchables and for the touchables. The republic is an empire of the Hindus over the untouchables. It is a kind of colonialism of the Hindus designed to exploit the untouchables. The untouchables have no rights; they are there only to wait, serve and submit. They are there to do or to die. They have no rights because they are outside the village republic and because they are outside the so-called republic, they are outside the Hindu-fold. This is a vicious circle.

Dhiru Bhai Sheth is of the opinion that race and caste are two separate issues that need to be addressed in different ways. It is, therefore, inappropriate to view caste from the racial angle.

However, race and caste may be recognised as two sides of the same coin. Rigid social sanctions are developed in both the caste system and among races in opposition though we have no definite measure of rigidity so that one cannot say whether the rigidity is less in the racial system in the USA or more in the caste system in India. However, in the caste system, each caste knows or assumes that it knows its place. The very nature of racial opposition, however, precludes attainment of such a degree of adjustment. The poet pictures some of this indecision thus:

My old man's a white old man,
And my old mother's black.
My old man died in a fine big house,
My ma died in a shack,
I wonder where I'm gonna die,
Being neither white nor black?

Also, where rigidity in the racial/caste order is concerned, it is to be noted that inter-racial or caste mixture through inter-marriages has been more a feature of the Indian society than the American context. A certain amount of equilibrium has been achieved between castes in Indian society. The whites in America, however, still regard the blacks as those whose forefathers were brought in as slaves to serve the white population or as second-class citizens who have come in search of employment.

Years ago Booker T. Washington recognised the race problem in the USA very clearly. In India, Ambedkar recognised the roots of the caste system and casteism. The race as well as caste problems assume different dimensions from decade to decade, and the issue tends to become more and more challenging in both the countries. However, the basic truth is that the idea of the blacks and the dalits is that they should not be identified with the worst type of slavery and as bonded labourers. They want to be workers, ministers, doctors, or teachers without any distinction on the basis of their colour and caste.

Robert E. Lane asked Johnson about the main problem facing America. Mr. Johnson said, "Well, I think a race problem—more so—is coming up more so ..... I think that is a serious (problem) and will be quite serious as time goes on."[13] If the same question is asked of anyone in India, anyone will say that India is facing the caste problem. But if everyone tries to remove racism and casteism in America and India respectively, there would be less and less discrimination between whites and blacks in America and between high caste Hindus and dalits in India.

Sixty years ago, Gunnar Myrdal concluded that "the American Negro problem is a problem in the heart of the American." 'The black problem' is not just a white man's problem; it is a black man's as well, because of what white prejudice and discrimination have done to the black's personality and self-esteem.

Actually, the racial trouble in America and the caste-based exploitation in India started centuries ago when the white men and the upper castes began to treat black men and the shudras and untouchables as inferiors, and they have not stopped yet. A major part of the problem lies in what these centuries have done to the victims' personality: they have learnt in early childhood about the stigma attached to colour/caste.

The oppressed race or caste is unable to take its place in the mainstream until the oppressed stop despising themselves. They will be unable to compete on equal terms until they are able to purge from their minds all sense of racial or caste-based superiority and inferiority, until they really believe, with all of one's being, that they are free men, and act accordingly. In this sense, therefore, only the victimised group can solve its problem. For freedom and equality, like power, cannot be given or handed down as a gift. They must be taken by people unwilling to settle for anything less.

On the other hand, prejudice will disappear only when a considerable majority of the whites/Hindus are convinced that they have nothing to fear from close, daily association with the blacks/dalits in jobs, school and neighborhoods. Everyone who feels moved by the deplorable condition of the untouchables begins by saying: "We must do something for the untouchables." One seldom hears any of the persons interested in the problem saying: "Let us do something to change the Hindu." It is invariably assumed that the object to be reclaimed is the untouchable as though untouchability was due to his depravity and he alone is responsible for his condition. If there is to be a mission, it must be for the untouchables. Nothing requires to be done to the Hindu. He is sound in mind, manners and morals. He is whole, there is nothing wrong with him. He is not the sinner.

What is the real state of affairs? This argument that there is nothing wrong with the Hindu and that the untouchable is responsible for whatever wrong he suffers is very much an argument that is used by the Christians for defending themselves against the inhuman treatment accorded by them to the Jews.[14] A very crushing reply has been given by Louis Goulding to the Christians on behalf of the suffering Jews. In discussing the source of the Jewish problem we should read Louis Goulding.[15]

If we equate Paddy with the Hindu and scotch terrier with the untouchable the argument of Goulding will apply to the Hindus no less than it does to the Christians. If for the reasons given by Goulding the Jewish problem is in reality a Christian problem then the problem of the untouchables is primarily a Hindu problem.

Are the Hindus conscious, do they recognise that the untouchables are a problem to them? Are they worried about it? The untouchables do not belong to the society of the Hindus and the Hindu does not feel that he and the untouchable belong to one society. This is the reason why the conduct of the Hindu is marked by a moralistic unconcernedness.

Not having a conscience, the Hindu has no such thing in him as righteous indignation against the inequalities and injustices and refuses to budge. By his absence of conscience the Hindu is a great obstacle in the path of the removal of untouchability.

Comparing untouchability with apartheid, while speaking at a function in Town Hall organised by the Martin Luther King Society to celebrate the anniversary of Gandhi's birth, defence minister said that a brahmin could not be distinguished from a 'bhangi' (of the sweeper class) on the basis of appearance. The same applied to a Muslim and a Hindu, while the contrast between a black and a white was quite obvious. And yet the prejudices in this country are as terrible as in the USA.[16]

The movements started by King and Ambedkar for improving the condition of the downtrodden–the blacks in America and the dalits in Indian society respectively–hold a special place in the history of racial and caste relations. They emerged as champions for the cause of the exploited in their society at a time when the people needed their leadership the most: while, on the one hand, the blacks had been held in bondage by the white power for centuries, the high-caste Hindus, on the other, had been oppressing the dalits since ancient times. In the chapters that follow a detailed study has been made regarding their education, influences, beliefs and their struggle on the social and political fronts.

Notes

1. The paper was prepared for presentation to the national seminar on Marx, Ambedkar and Polarisation of Oppressed and Exploited Classes in India, 1991, sponsored by Sanjivayya Institute of Socio-Economic Studies, New Delhi.
2. Williams, Sir Monier, *Hinduism*, Society for Promoting Christian Knowledge, London, 1894, pp. 1–12.
3. Samagra Tilak (Marathi), Kesari Mudranalaya, Pune, 1976, vol. 6, p. 791.
4. Kshirsagar, R.K., *Dalit Movement in India and its Leaders*, M.D. Publications Pvt. Ltd., New Delhi, 1994, p.13.
5. Cox, Oliver C., *Caste, Class and Race*, Modern Reader Paperbacks, New York, 1948, p. 298.
6. Parsons, Talcott, *Societies and Evolutionary and Comparative Perspectives*, Harvard University, 1966, p. 78.
7. Kavlaekar Kashinath, *Non-Brahmin Movement in Southern India: 1873–1949*, Shivaji University Press, Kolhapur, 1979, p.1.
8. Kshirsagar, R.K., op cit., p.19.
9. Hingorani, A.T., *My Philosophy of Life by Mahatma Gandhi*, 1961, p. 161.
10. Report of the Committee (1969), p. 1.
11. "Hindus and their want of Social Conscience", Dr. Baba Saheb Ambedkar, *Writings and Speeches*, vol.5, Education Department, Maharashtra, Bombay, 1989.
12. Lane, R.E., *Political Ideology*, The Free Press of Glencoe, New York, 1962.
13. Ibid.
14. "Hindus and their Want of Social Conscience", Dr. Baba Saheb Ambedkar, *Writings and Speeches*, vol.5, Education Department Maharashtra, Bombay, 1989.
15. Mr. Louis says:

    I beg leave to give a very homely instance of the sense in which I consider the Jews problem in essence a Gentile problem. A close acquaintance of mine has a certain Irish terrier of mixed pedigree, the dog Paddy, who is to my friend John Smith as the apple of both his eyes. Paddy dislikes scotch terriers, it is enough for one to pass within twenty yards of

Paddy for him to deafen the neighbourhood with challenges and insults. It is a practice which John Smith deplores, which, therefore, he does his best to check—all the more as the objects of Paddy's detestation are often inoffensive creatures who seldom speak first. Despite all his affection for Paddy, he considers as I do, that Paddy's unmannerly behaviour is due to some measure of original sin in Paddy. It has not yet been suggested to us that what is here involved is a scotch terrier problem and that when Paddy attacks a neighbour who is peacefully engaged in inspecting the evening smell it is the neighbour who should be arraigned for inciting to attack by the fact of his existence.

16. V.T. Rajshekhar, *Statesman*, Bangalore, October 3, 1978. This is an interesting observation since many black Americans believe that if they were assimilated and looked the same as the anglo-Americanised majority white population, the problem would be solved. This observation in India tells us that even a high degree of biological assimilation will not bring equality, when preceded by historical circumstances of slavery and apartheid.

3

King and Ambedkar: Their Childhood, Education, Influences and Religious Beliefs

Both Martin Luther King and B.R. Ambedkar, at a young age, came to learn of the inferior status attached to their lives and others of their community and the restrictions in inter-mixing imposed on them. The seed of a silent rebellion was thus laid at a tender age. As they grew up, the awareness that their people were being unjustly forced to undergo sufferings gave rise to a determination that they would mobilise the strength of their people into a mass revolution for social equality and justice. In their academic careers, they came across the views and thoughts of various philosophers and leaders, which they imbibed or even questioned to mould their ideas. Thus, on the one hand, their mind was kindled by the spirit of these great men and, on the other, their thinking minds emerged with original ideas. The religious beliefs of King and Ambedkar were similar in approach: they had the same faith in the absolute reality of the spirit that pervades the universe and in man's capacity to become one with it. Their thinking grew out of their experiences and influences and it was reflected in the socio-political programmes they launched to emancipate their downtrodden brethren from centuries of slavery and hardships. So we see that their socio-political programme was a constructive one that not only stressed integrating all blacks in America and dalits of India to demand equal rights and status but also involved reforms within these groups to bring self-reliance among their people and increase their ability to work together for a socially desirable goal.

It is hard to compare two great leaders as Martin Luther King and Baba Saheb Ambedkar but a comparative analysis brings out the similarity in their circumstances, background, academic career, influences and views.

King was a product of American democracy, idealised by the Jeffersonian proclamation that "all men are created equal". He believed that the "great glory of democracy is the right to protest for rights". However, King was disappointed to see the way democracy was functioning in America especially with respect to racial equality. He protested against the racial prejudices and oppression of his fellowmen by the white society. Ambedkar also revolted against caste-based prejudices. After studying the religious books he stated that the caste system in the Hindu society was undemocratic. He fought for radical reforms in Hinduism, revolting against its orthodox dogmas. According to him, untouchability was a grievous crime and unless it was uprooted, he said, "the whole society will destroy itself".

King, like Ambedkar, refused to believe that any human being could be inferior on the basis of his birth. He revolted against racism in America. He brought to light the simple fact that in many ways the church sanctioned slavery. He thought a religion true to its ideals should consider segregation morally wrong. To him segregation was conceived in pride, hatred and falsehood as well as in ignorance. He vehemently criticised the American churches for not opposing segregation and for not declaring it immoral. King not only brought the subject of segregation and conformism into his church, but, like Ambedkar, also took them into the street in the form of various protests against the injustices and prejudices of conforming America. What follows is a detailed comparative study of the life and beliefs of Martin Luther King and B.R. Ambedkar.

Background and Childhood

James Albert, Martin Luther King's paternal grandfather, was part-Irish and part-black. He was a share-cropper in Stock Bridge, a typical southern village, twenty miles from Atlanta. King's grandmother, Delia was all black, a very dark and well-built woman.

King's father, Martin Michael King, Sr., the second child of James and Delia, was born on December 19, 1899. The drudgery and degradation of plantation life made him leave Stock Bridge and go to Atlanta to look for better opportunities. Atlanta, like most southern towns, is doused in southern history. The black Atlantans considered the Yankee Army a liberation army, as they were set free by President Lincoln's Emancipation Proclamation in 1863 following the civil war. Though the blacks had become free they remained in a state of half-slavery for a long time. In Atlanta also, there was racial segregation. Churches and schools were segregated. Blacks and whites lived in two separate worlds.

On January 15, 1929, Martin Luther King, Jr. was born. There was nothing unusual in the birth. It was just the birth of another black child in the home of a self-made black minister. As a child Martin was healthy and fun-loving. His father was a strict disciplinarian. He wanted his children to have an orderly life—early to bed, early to rise. For King Sr. there was a time for everything—time to play, time to eat, time to pray. In the house, Martin, his sister Christine, and his brother Daniel were required to learn verses from the Bible for recitation before the evening meal.

He was originally named Michael Luther, but later changed his name to Martin in honour of the founder of Lutheran Church, a great leader of Christian reform in Europe during the eighteenth century.

Martin suffered painful experiences growing up as a black boy. Many day-to-day incidents revealed to him his miserable plight and white discrimination against his community. Once he was forbidden by the grocer's wife to play with her children as he was coloured (black). The boy felt depressed on knowing the meaning of being 'coloured'. In another incident, when he along with his father visited a shoe store in downtown Atlanta, they were asked to move to the seats in the rear if they wanted to be attended to. It not only angered them but also gave young Martin a new awareness of the segregation system in public places in the country.

Likewise, Bhim Rao Ambedkar was of humble origins. His family was poor as well as a victim of untouchability. Unlike King, he was born in a country ruled by a foreign power. Bhim Rao's grandfather came of a Mahar family from Ratangiri district. The Mahar community, one of the leading dalit communities, was considered intelligent and brave. The Mahars had formed the backbone of the Maratha army and had been the first to come in contact with the Europeans in India.

From the very commencement of the rule of the East India Company, Bhim Rao Ambedkar's father got the opportunity of military training and military career. It was because of the British practice of the recruitment of Mahars. Bhim Rao's grandfather was a retired military man. Ramji, Bhim Rao's father, rose to the rank of a Subedar Major and was a head instructor in a military school for about 14 years, and settled in Dapoli in Ratangiri after retirement. But later, he shifted to Satara and the family lived there till 1904.

The last of fourteen children, Bhim Rao was born at Mhow in central India in April 14, 1891. The family had a tough time living in poverty and had to do with a simple home in the dalit colony.

In contrast, King's father was educated as well as a rich person. He had a two-storey house with a spacious front porch. His father had business interests in Atlanta's several black-owned trades. He was the President of the local chapter of the National Association for the Advancement of Colored People (NAACP). He was also an activist while Ambedkar's father interacted in a limited sphere owing to his military background. Both were deeply religious as well as strict disciplinarians and considerably influenced their children. Both Ramji Sakpal and mother were deeply religious. It was during the British rule that India became a single political entity. Awakening among the dalits was increasing, especially as education was spreading among them. Ambedkar in early childhood had a lot of bitter experiences whether in school, or in the streets, or in the temple. At every step, he was victimised by dogmatised Hindus. But the strange thing was that neither was Ambedkar pushed back nor disappointed by such situations; he derived inspiration from them. At that time, unlike the dalits, the blacks, though discriminated on racial basis, had their own churches, schools and community halls. They were not scattered like the dalits in India. They lived together and had their own trade. They were financially better off than the dalits. But in spite of all these things, the blacks suffered from discrimination by whites at different levels and this included social segregration.

Ambedkar had a painful experience of untouchability during his stay at Satara. Once he along with his elder brother went to meet his father at Goregaon where he worked. They travelled up to Masur by train from where they had to take a bullock cart for Goregaon. Just after going a few yards from the Masur station the cartman who was a caste Hindu came to know that the boys in his cart were untouchables. He threw them out of the cart; but they persuaded the cartman to allow them to use the cart by paying double the fare with the cartman following on foot. Throughout the journey they were not able to drink water as people either pointed to a filthy water source or refused to give them drinking water. This was a rude shock to young Bhim. This incident made him realise the inhumanity of the system of untouchability.

The circumstances were the same in America as well as in India. The society of both countries was influenced by the rigidity in race and caste. For the parents it was tough. They had to tell their children that they were considered inferior for being coloured or untouchable, and were not allowed to play with the white children of other castes or go to certain places reserved for others. The mother had to tell her little child the sad story he could not comprehend. Nevertheless, the child obeyed thinking that it was the right thing to do because his mother asked him to do it that way.

Almost all the children felt inferior and their child egos got hurt when they began to learn the truth. As soon as the children discovered that they could not do things because of the colour of their skin or their caste, feelings of resentment developed in their young minds.

It is not that every child was told by its mother of the existing prejudices in society. Some of them came to learn about this at an early age, as we have seen, through their own personal experiences. In those days racial symbols and caste-discriminatory attitudes were so openly prevalent in the American and the Indian society respectively that all normal children could eventually perceive them. They observed segregation even where recreational facilities and the transportation system were concerned. Such observations contributed to the young child's attitude towards race/caste differences. They not only became aware of racial differences in terms of colour/caste differences, but also began to identify themselves in terms of race/caste.

Education

M.K. Baruah discusses the education of young Martin Luther King particularly his school environment and the problems encountered by him.[1] As he grew up, young King was enrolled in the elementary school. King liked school from the beginning. He was a good student and skipped three grades during the entire period of elementary and secondary education. Then, Martin attended the Laboratory High School in Atlanta for two years. Later on, he was transferred to Booker T. Washington High School where he completed his high school education. During his high school days, Martin occasionally used to sing before the congregation of Ebenezer and at church conventions, his favourite song being "I want to be more like Jesus". His mother accompanied him on the piano.

King Sr. had enough money, but that could not be wasted. He used to give weekly pocket money to his children, but that was not enough for the youngsters. The children used to earn extra pocket money by selling soft drinks or delivering newspapers. From his childhood, King was an emotional and hyper-sensitive boy. Twice he tried to commit suicide. Once, while sliding down the banister, his brother Alfred Daniel knocked their grandmother down. Grandmother became unconscious and young King thought she was dead. He went to the second floor of the house and jumped out of the window. The second time he attempted suicide was when he heard the news of his grandmother's death. King loved his grandmother dearly. Perhaps all this reflects a nine-year-old's fear of losing somebody very dear to him.

From the beginning King realised that his father would like to see him succeed. His father often used to remind the children of the harsh realities of the world. He also began to see with his own eyes how hard it was for a black to be successful in life. Nevertheless, he began to pursue his studies.

At school, the teacher encouraged free thinking among the students. Later Martin entered a private college at Morehouse and as such it was free from pressures that were always felt by state-supported black institutions. Students here mostly came from the south.

King's first contact with the white people is discussed in detail by M.K. Baruah.[2] It was when he became a member of Atlanta's Intercollegiate Students Association, the aim of which was to encourage fellowship among students of different colleges and to study common problems confronting students of the Atlanta area. "It was the most rewarding experience of my life," he recalled in later years.

> The wholesome relation we had in this group convinced me that we had many white persons as allies, particularly among the younger generation. I had been ready to resent the white race, but as I got to see more of the white people, my resentment was softened and a spirit of co-operation took its place.

His experiences in college involve an incident which took place during King's second year at Morehouse when he directly confronted white people in the segregated southern transportation. It was nothing but a usual black-white confrontation in southern buses that used to occur in those days. The incident undoubtedly left a deep impression on his young mind. For the first time he could understand the indignity with which a black had to travel in a southern bus. Perhaps this confrontation was partly responsible for his decision to assume the leadership of the Montgomery bus boycott in later days. The buses in Atlanta, Georgia were run on a first come, first serve basis, the blacks sitting from the back, the whites sitting from the front; both groups filling up seats towards the centre of the bus. King's family, especially King, Sr., in order to avoid the discourtesy of white drivers and the indignity of riding a segregated bus, never rode on them. However, Martin Luther King Jr. occasionally had to ride on one to get to school.

The incident took place when he was returning from Valdosta, Georgia, where he and a few other students had been taken by their speech teacher to participate in an elocution contest. Martin won the second prize in the contest and so it was a happy occasion for him. On his way home, a change of buses had to be made in Macon. The black students took the seats that were available. But when a few white people boarded the bus and had to remain standing as they could not find seats the driver asked the black students to vacate the seats for the white passengers. The students ignored this at first. However, the driver persisted and the students had to give up the seats eventually when their accompanying teacher, Miss Bradley, asked them to do so. Miss Bradley felt it was her duty to keep anything undesirable from happening.

Baruah notes that as the son of a prominent black minister in Atlanta, he could have had a white-collar job easily in some black-owned business. However, King chose to work as a labourer—one summer in a railway express company and another summer at a warehouse. He did this because he wanted to feel a sense of oneness with the masses and to understand their problems and hardships.[3]

In 1948, Martin graduated from Morehouse with sociology as his major. The Morehouse days were not perhaps his golden days of intellectual quest.

With an undergraduate degree in sociology, King left Atlanta in the August of 1948 to attend Crozer Theological Seminary at Chester, Pennsylvania, one of the more famous theological schools of the nation. A liberal rather than a denominational institution, to young King it was to turn out to be a wonderful experience studying in such an institution. Moreover, this was to be the first time that he would be attending college as a resident student.

The three-year course in Crozer was designed to provide students with thorough instructions in biblical, theological and other religious learning. The programme was also designed to give a good background of ethical and religious habits to those who chose either the career of ministry or that of missionary. In the first year, a student studied history and criticism of the Bible; in the second year, church history and the life and works of major prophets; and in the third year, philosophy of religion, ethics and social philosophy. There were only a few black students in the seminary in those days.

This was the first time King was studying with white students. At first a little nervous, his nervousness disappeared as he adjusted himself to his new environment. He immediately began to concentrate on his studies with a strong determination. Conscious of the fact that the general stereotypical impression of the whites was that blacks were dirty, lacking in manners and irregular. King always used to dress well with his shoes perfectly shined. He was never a minute late for class. Regular and conscientious in his studies, young King topped the class in almost all subjects. This gave him a new confidence, which coupled with his desire to understand the underlying causes of social evils turned his attention to serious intellectual pursuits.

Ambedkar was equally sensitive as King in his young days and he was made aware of the harsh realities of life for the untouchable castes. As he was dalit, he had to suffer the effects of casteism in his day-to-day life just as King had to undergo daily torment for being a black. Even the barber refused to cut his hair and his sister cut his hair. Such insulting ill-treatment was experienced by all dalits.

The school environment for Ambedkar was not similar to the environment in which King got educated. The dalit children were not encouraged to think and develop freely. Being a dalit, Ambedkar was forced to sit apart in the school. He could not mix with other boys or play with them. Even the teachers would not touch his note books. When he felt thirsty in the school, someone, perhaps the peon, opened the tap for water. He was not permitted to touch the tap as they believed he would pollute it. Sometimes, the peon was absent and then Ambedkar had to go without water. Thirsty, he returned to his house and only then could he quench his thirst.[4] This was the kind of humiliating and inhuman treatment he suffered at the hands of his teachers and other staff in his school. Thomas

Mathew writes: "The conditions in the school were much oppressive. The Sanskrit teacher refused to teach him Sanskrit. And Bhim was forced to take Persian as the second language in high school."[5] In spite of all discriminations he became, like King, very diligent in his studies.

In 1904, the family of Ambedkar shifted to Bombay and Bhim Rao Ambedkar joined the Elphinstone high school, where he continued his high school education. Here too he had to suffer insults and discrimination on account of the varna system. The treatment outside the school was no better. In 1907, he completed his matriculation. This was a great achievement for a dalit and the event was celebrated by his community. According to Kuber,[6] a boy from Mahar family passing the matriculation examination was an admirable feat.

Ambedkar had a thirst for more education and greater knowledge. He had no facilities but there was an urge in his heart for education. Overcoming all obstacles Ambedkar pursued single-mindedly the goal of acquiring a thorough education. It was his conviction that education would unlock the doors of opportunity and advancement for the depressed classes and their backward sections. "Without knowledge there can be no power" he maintained till the end of his life.[7] With a scholarship from Maharaja Sayajirao of Baroda, he took admission in college. Here also he had to contend with a hostile environment. He concentrated his energies on his studies and passed his BA examination in 1912 with English and Persian as his subjects.

W.N. Kuber examines the educational opportunities that came Ambedkar's way and the course of his academic career.[8] The death of his father on 2 February 1913 was a shock to him. His father, Ramji, had sacrificed much to provide education to his son and had incurred debts. It was unfortunate that he did not live to see his son go abroad for higher education.

A new opportunity came to Ambedkar when the Maharajah of Baroda thought of sending some students to the Columbia University, USA for higher studies. Ambedkar was one of the students selected. On June 4, 1913, he joined Columbia University as a Gaekwad scholar. He was the first Mahar to study in a foreign university. This was a unique opportunity for an Indian and especially for dalits.

In USA, Ambedkar joined a cosmopolitan club where some of the Indian students lived. He could move freely. He could conduct his daily routine with a status of equality. He found it a new world. It helped him to enlarge his mental vision. Professor Seligman, the well-known economist, was his teacher. In June 1915, he obtained the M.A. degree for his thesis, "Ancient Indian Commerce". In May 1916, he read a paper on "The Castes in India, their Mechanism, Genesis, and Development" at the anthropology seminar sponsored by Dr. Goldenweiser. It was published in the *Indian Antiquary* in May 1917. It was also published in the form of a brochure, the first published work of Ambedkar. Therein, he observed that endogamy is the essence of castes. According to him, a caste was an enclosed class and it existed before Manu whom he described as an audacious person, a daredevil. According to him, Manu simply codified the existing caste rules.

Lala Lajpat Rai, the great nationalist leader, was then in exile in America. He used to go daily to the college library where Ambedkar studied. Lalaji enquired about this Indian student. He found that this Indian student was a Mahar. Lalaji was as radical in social reforms as he was in politics. He discussed with Ambedkar the national struggle for independence which was going on in India. In June 1916, Ambedkar submitted his thesis for the degree of Ph.D. entitled "National Dividend for India: A Historic and Analytical Study". It was published eight years afterwards under the title, *The Evolution of Provincial Finance in British India*. The original doctoral dissertation was revised in the light of the

Montague-Chelmsford Reforms with reference to finance. The book was dedicated to Maharajah Sayajirao and it had an introduction by Professor S.A. Seligman. Seligman stated therein: "Nowhere to my knowledge has such a detailed study of the underlying principles been made." In the thesis Ambedkar stated that the whole policy was dictated by the interests of British industries and manufacturers. He concluded that in every country there is social oppression and social injustice. This does not mean that the country should be without political power. This book was so indispensable that during the budget session Indian legislators used this as a reference book, and to students it became a guide. When he was called to give evidence before the Hilton-Young Commission on Indian currency, he saw with pride that every member of the commission had this book for reference.

Ambedkar left Columbia University to join the London School of Economics and Political Science as a graduate student in June 1916. Seligman gave him introductory letters to Professor Cannan and Sydney Webb. In October 1916, he was admitted to Gray's Inn for law. But he faced a crisis when he had to return to India after spending a year in London working on a thesis for the M.Sc. (Economics) degree. The return was owing to termination of the scholarship granted to him by Maharajah Sayajirao of Baroda. Ambedkar tried to persuade him to reconsider his decision but without success. He obtained permission of the London University through the recommendation of Professor Cannan to resume his studies within a period not exceeding four years from October, 1917.

In the course of the three years from 1920 to 1923, he completed his thesis on the problem of the rupee, for which the University of London awarded him a D.Sc. Before leaving England he spent three months in Germany, where he was engaged in further studies in economics at the University of Bonn.

From 1913 to 1917 and again from 1920 to 1923 Ambedkar was in the West, and when at the age of thirty-two he finally returned to the country of his birth it was as one of the most highly qualified men in public life.

Influences

At Crozer Theological Seminary, Martin Luther King Jr. began to read the basic teachings of all the great philosophers. M.K. Baruah explains the influence of Hegel, Rauschenbusch, Plato, Aristole, Rousseau, Bentham, Mill and Locke on the thinking of King: he not only agreed with many of their thoughts and imbibed them but also argued against some of their contentions, giving an analysis of his own. King was impressed by Hegel's study of the dialectical process and his idea of the progress of growth through struggle and pain and developed a rational, philosophical approach in reflecting on any question. Rauschenbusch's works helped him understand the roots of social problems. He was stimulated by Plato and Aristotle's rule of reason and the philosophy of reforms of Mill and Bentham for building up an ideal society. However, he also questioned Hegel's contention that universal reason gained its height in a society of free individuals, each subordinating individual reason to the universal reason. He did not share Rauschenbusch's optimism about human nature and disagreed with him in identifying the church with a particular social and economic system. Overall, the divergent views of the philosophers he studied laid the foundations of an emerging personal philosophy in him which was to flower in his later days. He began to realise that to improve the individual socio-economic condition of the blacks, it was imperative to improve their collective lot. He now began to dream of an American society where blacks and whites would live with equal status, where both would share the wealth of the society (see Annexure 6).

During his second year at Crozer in 1949, King for the first time read Karl Marx and Lenin. He read Marx's *Das Capital* and *Communist Manifesto*. According to their theory, as King understood it, the individual member had no individual existence, he received life and all his ideas from the society. Thus Marxism demanded absolute subordination of the individual to his class. The individual is a microcosmic cell—meaningless outside the social body. He is a little stone in the monolithic mass of society. He is like a piece of clay to be moulded by the imprint of his group. Valid ideas are only those of the group as a whole: of the people, of the nation or of the class. All the arts too—music, painting, poetry, fiction, architecture and sculpture—are good only insofar as they express the society or class. This philosophy, to King, was basically subjective.

King rejected Marx's materialistic interpretation of history. As a Christian and a religious man who believed in the creative personal power in the universe, King rejected communism because there was no place for God or for religion in it; secondly, it advocated violence; and thirdly, it took away the freedom of spiritual life. He could not accept the metaphysical materialism and ethical relativism of communism. But though he opposed communism, he recognised some truths in it which tallied with the Christian view of some things. Communism advocated principles of social justice for all oppressed humanity. It grew as a protest against the privileged by the underprivileged. Perusal of Karl Marx's works gave him an understanding of the shortcomings of American capitalism. Capitalism created different classes and made exploitation of the poor and the powerless possible as the gap between the rich and the poor increased. People here were taught to be more concerned about making money than about leading a good life; to measure everything in terms of money. Capitalism or free enterprise led to practical materialism which, according to him, was "as deficient as the materialism taught by the communists".

He found that communism challenged the conscience of the American church which was unmindful towards the existing social problems in the country. King thought that it also challenged the whole system of American government that had not been able to solve the plight of the poor, nor the problem of the growing rate of underemployment and unemployment among blacks; nor had it been able to provide the much required housing facilities for ghetto-dwellers in spite of the country's manifold rise in terms of the gross national product.

Frederick Nietzsche was a philosopher whom King read with much interest, particularly his books *Genealogy of Morals* and *The Will to Power* but Nietzsche failed to make an impact on King for various reasons. To Nietzsche, the Christian concept of love, suffering, humility, piety were nothing but a glorification of weakness. Study of Nietzsche momentarily disappointed the young minister who was going to preach Christ's love in the future. However, King was soon to see that Nietzsche's 'will to power' theory was based on his contempt for ordinary morals which did not appeal to King.

The Indian Influence on King

King's visit to India came at a later stage of his life when he was deep into the political movement for black equality and had come to be recognised as a leading black civil rights leader worldwide. After the success of the Montgomery bus struggle, he made a trip to India with his wife Corretta and close friend, Reddick to gain first-hand experiences of India—a country which had successfully waged a non-violent, peaceful struggle for independence from the British.

King had become convinced by this time that it was through the Gandhian method of *satyagraha* that his greatest dream—to achieve racial equality for the black Americans—could be realised. King held a non-violent attitude even in his youth. He liked to wrestle, but he himself never struck anyone.

Once Martin was kicked by a schoolboy for not moving quickly enough to let him pass. Martin did not strike back. On another occasion, he was accused and slapped by a white woman for stepping on her feet. However, Martin did not say or do a thing.

Now he was determined to apply fully the Gandhian concept of *satyagraha* (non-violence) with a new vigour in the American scene. King thought that an early trip to India would definitely help him understand the tactics of non-violence fully.

Although King was impressed by many aspects of Indian life and culture, he was surprised to notice the extreme poverty of the general Indian masses. He was really dismayed and wondered how such extreme poverty could exist in a democratic country like India where the government instituted so many social programmes.

King was impressed by Nehru's statement that Indians could not think of talking about refusing to discriminate against untouchables without thinking somehow of doing something and taking some responsibility to lift the standards of the people who have been exploited for so long. Nehru had said that there could be a little discrimination in reverse—giving them something that others are not given—in order to atone for exploiting these people for thousands of years.

It is, however, surprising that we have no detailed descriptions of his meeting with dalit leaders, writers and politicians—which would only have been appropriate in the context of the struggles that were going on in America and India.

Ambedkar, like King, was much influenced by the religious and social philosophy of great men and leaders. Kuber discusses the influences on Ambedkar, stating that he regarded three great men as his preceptors. The first was Kabir, the second was Jyotiba Phooley and the third was the Buddha. Kabir impressed him with his Bhakti cult philosophy; Phooley inspired him to strive against brahminism and for amelioration of the masses, their education and economic upliftment; and the Buddha gave him mental and metaphysical satisfaction and showed the way leading to the emancipation of the dalits through the path of mass conversion.

Influence of the West on Ambedkar

Unlike King who visited India while being deeply involved in his political struggle, Ambedkar's years spent in the West were at an early stage of his career—during the course of his academic pursuits in the West's noted universities.

Ambedkar was impressed by two important things. These were, firstly, the Fourteenth Amendment to the Constitution of the USA, which gave freedom to the blacks, and secondly, the life of Booker T. Washington who died in 1915. Booker Washington was a great social reformer and educator of the black race in America. He was the founder and president of the Tuskegee Institute which disseminated education among the blacks and broke the shackles of bondage which had crushed the blacks for centuries.

Ambedkar realised that the West could influence Indian social and political life in a positive manner. He was of the view that this Western system alone could break the shackles of the untouchables in India. He preached, by his own example, that 'worth' and not 'birth' shapes the life of an individual in any country. Before he entered Indian politics he was fully equipped with the western thought of democracy, equality, liberty and fraternity. His study in England and America fully revealed to him that the Hindu social system would never free the untouchable from social and political oppression. It became clear to him that not the law of Manu but constitutional safeguards would ultimately lead dalits to a free life.

Religious Ideas

Both King and Ambedkar were deeply religious men. They had the same vision sustained by the same faith in the absolute reality of the spirit that pervades this universe and in the capacity of man to realise his oneness with it. Both strove, each in his own way, to attain this ideal. Neither of them sought God in the privacy of the temple or church, nor did they follow traditional religious ways to reach Him. Both had the same logical mind and the courage, willingness and capacity to suffer.

These two leaders greatly influenced the world in the foundation of a new society—a society not based on a totalitarian concept but a truly democratic society. They advocated world federalism, leading mankind to a true unity of brotherhood. They preached universalism in religion. M.K. Baruah explains that King was not only a born Christian but also a Christian minister who was devoted to the creed of Christ and was true to his religion. Early in his life, he became aware of the existing dogmas of Christianity. But to him, the Christian gospel, on the one hand, sought to change the soul of man and thereby unite it with God and, on the other hand, "sought to change the environmental conditions of man, so that the soul would have a chance after it changed". He pointed out to the church the existing racial prejudice in American society. Urging American Christians and the American churches to get rid of the cancer of segregation, King said in one of his sermons, "Paul's Letter to American Christians":

> I understand that there are Christians among you who try to find biblical bases to justify segregation and argue that the Negro is inferior by nature. Oh, my friends, this is blasphemy and against everything the Christian religion stands for. I must repeat what I have said to many Christians before, that in Christ there is neither Jew nor Greek, there is neither bond

> nor free, there is neither male nor female: for ye are all one in Christ Jesus. Moreover, I must reiterate the words I uttered on Mars Hill: "God that made the world and all things therein ... hath made of one blood all nations of men for to dwell on all the face of the earth." So, Americans, I must urge you to be rid of every aspect of segregation. Segregation is a blatant denial of the unity which we have in Christ. It substitutes an 'I-it' relationship for the 'I-thou' relationship, and relegates persons to the status of things. It scars the soul and degrades the personality. It inflicts the segregated with a false sense of inferiority, while confirming the segregator in a false estimate of his own superiority. It destroys community and makes brotherhood impossible. The underlying philosophy of Christianity is diametrically opposed to the underlying philosophy of racial segregation. I hope the churches of America will play a significant role in conquering segregation. It has always been the responsibility of the church to broaden horizons and challenge the status quo. The church must move out into the arena of social action.

King was of the view that the segregated never meet in God. Segregation is established on pride and falsehood. It is unbrotherly and impersonal. Segregation denies the sacredness of human personality.

Baruah points out that King was the preacher who tried to revolt against the prevailing racism in America but with some limitations. He was not a preacher-politician in the context of that segregation, the racial issue, which is also a political issue in America. He was simply a preacher as well as a social reformer. He was a spiritual man and believed in God and soul.

W.N. Kuber[9] explains Ambedkar's conception of religion according to which religion was the driving force of human activity and its foundations were essential to life and society. For Ambedkar, religion was a part of one's 'social inheritance'. He wanted religion, but he did not want hypocrisy in the name of religion. He remarked:

> Man cannot live by bread alone. He has a mind which needs food for thought.

Ambedkar felt that religion had to be judged by social standards, based on social ethics.[10] He linked religion with the social being of the people. He remarked: "The religion which discriminates between two followers is partial and the religion which treats crores of its adherents worse than dogs and criminals and inflicts upon them insufferable disabilities is no religion at all."[11] For at that time, the dalits were segregated and humiliated by the caste Hindus in not only the social but also the religious sense. As Baudh scholar Sangharakshita notes, the religious disabilities of the untouchables related mainly to what became known, in modern times, as 'temple entry'[12]. Untouchables were not permitted to enter Hindu temples or even, in some cases, to work along a street in which a Hindu temple was situated. So the dalits built their own temples in which they worshipped either the popular Hindu gods and goddesses or quasi-dalit and tribal divinities specific to their community. Brahmins did not, of course, officiate in these temples. Dalits were also prohibited from studying the scriptures, especially the *Vedas* and from engaging in the practice of asceticism (*tapasya*).

Ambedkar wanted to have a religion in the sense of 'spiritual principles' truly 'universal' applicable to all times, to all countries and to all races.[13] He gave four characteristics of religion: (1) Religion in the sense of morality, must, therefore, remain the governing principle in every society. (2) Religion, if it is to function, must be in accord with reason which is merely another name for science. (3) Its moral code must recognise the fundamental tenets of liberty, equality and fraternity. Unless a religion recognises these three fundamental principles of social life, religion will be doomed. (4) Religion must not sanctify or ennoble poverty.[14] But Hinduism, for him, was "a mass of sacrificial, social, political and sanitary rules and regulations, all mixed up."[15]

He said, "what is called religion by Hindus is nothing but a multitude of commands and prohibitions."[16] He enumerated the evils of Hindu religion as follows: (1) it has deprived moral life of freedom; (2) it has only conformity to commands; and (3) the laws are iniquitous in that they are not the same for one class as for another. He concluded that this religion must be destroyed and there was nothing irreligious in working for the destruction of such a religion.[17]

Ambedkar wanted Hinduism to change itself from a 'religion of rules' to a 'religion of principles', a change required before it could be called a 'true religion'. Among his requirements were: "(1) one standard book of Hindu religion; (2) no hereditary priesthood, but an examination system open to all; (3) state sanads (permits) required for priests; (4) a limit by law on the number of priests; (5) state supervision of the priests' morals, beliefs and worship."[18]

Finally, however, the behaviour of caste-Hindus who continued to inflict sufferings upon the dalits led Ambedkar to decide in favour of renouncing Hinduism and getting converted to Buddhism along with his followers. The insulting treatment at the hands of the Hindus; the denial of Sanskrit and Vedic learning; his experiences in Baroda and in the Bombay bar—all these convinced him that the dalit would never receive just treatment in Hindu dharma and Hindu society. He was sure that individual and group mobility were difficult for the untouchable within the Hindu social system. He was aware that compassion, equality and freedom were not to be found in Hindu religion. He rejected renunciation. He was attracted towards Buddhism because of its moral basis of equality, justice and its wide basis of humanitarianism.

In the All Bombay District Mahar Conference, May 30–31, 1936, Ambedkar characterised the problem of untouchability as a problem of class strife. It was a strife between two societies; the Hindus and the dalits. He thought that to remain in Hinduism and attempt to abolish the caste system was like sweetening poison. To abolish the caste exploitation he emphasised that they must look for power from some source outside the Hindu fold.

Ambedkar's journey to Buddhism can be traced over a span of forty years. Ambedkar's first recorded contact with Buddhism occurred in 1908, when he was sixteen. He had just passed the matriculation exam and his community celebrated the occasion with a public meeting in his honour. Among the chief guests were S.K. Bole, Krishnsi Arsun Keluskar and others. Keluskar presented a copy of *Life of the Buddha* which was published in Marathi, to the young Ambedkar.

Madhu Limye writes that after a long time Ambedkar made a provocative speech at the Presidency Depressed Classes Conference at Yevale in Nasik district in November 1935. Ambedkar then said that he felt that the depressed classes were treated in a horrible way because they called themselves Hindus. If they had been members of another faith none would have dared to treat them as pariahs. He, therefore, called upon them to choose any religion which would give them "equality of status and treatment."[19]

The effects of Ambedkar's declaration were immediate and far-reaching. Meetings were held throughout the country by various interested parties, and statements and counter-statements were made. At the same time, K.L. Gutta, a Muslim leader, telegraphed to Ambedkar saying that the whole of Muslim India was ready to welcome and honour him and the dalits and promised full political, social, economic and religious rights to them. The same offer was made by the Nizam of Hyderabad, the richest man in the world, who was willing to give a sum of forty or fifty million rupees if he would undertake to convert the dalits to Islam. It is reported that many bishops and Sikh leaders approached Ambedkar for conversion to the Christian and the Sikh religion respectively. Meanwhile, Ambedkar was taking the whole issue seriously. In 1945 he attended a Buddhist conference. On June 20, 1946, on behalf of People's Education Society, he started a college and named it Siddharth College. In 1948, he wrote a foreword to L. Narasu's book, *The Essence of Buddhism*. In 1950, he took part in the first Modern Buddhist Procession in Delhi. In December 1954, he took part in the Third World Federation of Buddhists. It is said that it was there that he made up his mind to embrace Buddhism. Ambedkar was inclined towards Buddhism openly from May 1956. On May 24 1956, he declared on the day of Buddha Jayanti celebrations at Nare Park in Bombay that he would embrace Buddhism in October 1956. On September 23 1956, he issued a press note announcing that his conversion to Buddhism would take place at Nagpur on the Dussara day October, 14, 1956 between 9 and 11 a.m. He himself preferred Nagpur which was a historic town where the Buddhist Nagas flourished in ancient times. D.C. Ahir claimed that due to Ambedkar's influence as the architect of India's Constitution, the Asoka Chakra (the wheel of law) was put on the flag of India, and the lions from the Asoka pillar at Sarnath were adopted as the national emblem.[20]

When Ambedkar resolved to renounce Hinduism, many asked the question: why had he waited for a long period of twenty years? It is said that he deliberately waited up to the 2500th birthday of Buddha. B.S. Murthy answered this question. He remarked, "The only answer seems to be that he dearly loved all that was best in Hinduism."[21]

Ambedkar recognised merits in Buddhist religion and philosophy that made it superior in comparison to Hinduism. He saw it as a true religion as it led to a life guided by the principles of knowledge, right path and compassion (see Annexure 7).

After his conversion to Buddhism on October 14, 1956, Ambedkar said that by discarding the ancient religion which stood for inequality and oppression, he was reborn and felt as if liberated from hell.[22] He was deeply moved when he said, "I renounce Hinduism". He reminded his followers of his vow taken in 1935 that "even though I am born a Hindu I will not die a Hindu". He fulfilled his vow. He had the satisfaction of having accomplished a great deed in establishing the revival of Buddhism in India.

One important point was that the Buddhist conversion released him from his place in the Hindu hierarchy and, from his point of view, gave him a new identity. S. Kharat remarked that "the aim of conversion is not economic but psychological". The untouchables began to think that they had a separate identity. Faith in Ambedkar helped in the growth of the conversion movement. According to Nehru, "Buddha functioned to some extent as a social revolutionary". This appealed to the untouchable most.

According to Issacs, "Ambedkar's choice of Buddhism was, in essence, a compromise with his sense of nationality". He used to say, "I belong to this nation—India. I am an Indian". He thought that Buddhism was indigenous. He had full faith in the integrity and oneness of India. He said that by conversion he has taken care not to bring any harm to the Indian culture and Indian historical traditions. Buddhism is purely Indian and Gautama Buddha is upholder of liberty not only of India but of the whole world. Hindus also shared in common the cultural heritage of Buddhism. According to Ambedkar, Hinduism and Buddhism differed in three vital aspects. In Hindu religion, there was *ishwar* (God), *atma* (Soul), and varna system; in Buddhism there was no *ishwar*, soul and caste or varna system.[23]

Their Social and Political Programmes

The most important part of the social and political programmes of both King and Ambedkar was the constructive measures advocated. Students Non-Violent Coordinating Committee, under the guidance of King, introduced constructive reforms for the Negro masses. These included a programme of political education for voter registration, citizenship education programme, writing clinics, and Operation Bread Basket. These programmes were designed to educate Negroes and to help initiate reforms in the existing social, political and economic institutions. They were to teach, inspire and encourage the underprivileged black masses to inspire them with visions of freedom, and to assist thousands of blacks in finding a sense of dignity and worth through self-reliance, economic independence and increased political participation.

Like King, Ambedkar devised a constructive programme towards sustaining a high level of morals among the dalits. It was a long-term plan for changes in existing social, political and economic institutions relating to education, respect for dalits, backwards' and womens' rights and development of their livelihood. The purpose of such a programme was to bring self-reliance to the people and increase their ability to work together for a socially desirable goal. Ambedkar thought that when oppressed people co-operate towards achieving a common aim through constructive reforms, they inevitably acquire valuable training for the kind of large scale co-operation that would be required in an active struggle against the oppressors.

Both King and Ambedkar wanted to begin reforms from within. King said: "Let us examine the reason given by white men for segregation.... Some say we want our constitutional rights so that we can marry their daughters. But that is nonsense, so we do not have to pay any attention to that. Some say, we smell. Well, the fact is that some of us do smell. We cannot afford a plane trip to Paris to buy the world's most expensive perfumes, but no Negro in Montgomery is so poor that he cannot afford a five cent bar of soap!" Without the slightest pretension, King went on to list all the drawbacks of his people—their laziness, illegitimacy rate, crime rate and the fault of spending beyond their means. No doubt these were partly legacies left behind by slavery. Ambedkar, likewise, stated that they could begin by cleaning up their homes, teaching the illiterate and providing schools for children of the poor.

Notes

1. Baruah, M.K., *Portrait of a Gandhian: Biography of Dr. Martin Luther King Jr.*, Gauhati, 1985, p. 33.
2. Ibid., p. 36.
3. Ibid., p. 40.
4. Bhagwan Das (ed.), *Thus spoke Ambedkar,* Jalandhar, 1977, vol. II, p. 162.
5. Mathew, Thomas, *Ambedkar: Reform or Revolution*, Segment Books, New Delhi, 1997, p. 2.
6. Kuber, W.N., *B.R. Ambedkar*, Publications Division, New Delhi, 1987, p. 14.
7. B.G. Kunte, comp, *Source Material on Dr. Baba Saheb Ambedkar and the Movement of Untouchables.*, Bombay, 1982, vol. 1, p. 234.
8. Kuber, W.N., op. cit., p. 20.
9. Ibid.
10. Ambedkar, *Annihilation of Caste*, p. 25.
11. Keer, Dhananjay, *Mahatma Jyotirao Phooley: Father of Social Revolution*, Popular Prakashan, Bombay, 1965.
12. Sangharakshita, *Ambedkar and Buddhism*, Windhorse Publications, Glasgow, 1986, p. 37.
13. Ambedkar, op. cit., p.71.
14. *Buddha and the Future of Religion*, paras 17–20.
15. Ibid. p. 73.
16. Ambedkar, op. cit., p. 72.

17. Ibid., pp. 73–74.
18. Ambedkar, op. cit., pp. 74–75.
19. Limaye, Madhu, *Prime Movers: Role of the Individual in History*, Samgam Books Limited, London, 1987.
20. Ahir, D.C., *Buddhism and Ambedkar*, p. 1985.
21. Murthy, B.S., *Depressed and Oppressed*, p. 185.
22. Letters to Gaekwad, p. 340.
23. W.N. Kuber, *Builders of Modern India: B.R. Ambedkar*, Publications Division, New Delhi, p. 84.

4

King and Ambedkar: The Struggle for Emancipation

Both Martin Luther King and B.R. Ambedkar were aware that only a mass revolution could bring about a transformation in the status of the oppressed people and this required a process combining political activity with reforms in society. Based on non-violence and disapproving the slogan of militant 'black power', King worked to build popular support for his efforts. It was the Montgomery bus boycott in 1955 that first threw the spotlight on King. From then on, he was prominent in the civil rights struggle, being in the forefront in the Washington March of 1966. His contributions were recognised and he was honoured with the Nobel Peace Prize. Ambedkar, similarly, beginning his struggle at an early age, conducted political activity for emancipation of the dalits with whole-hearted commitment. He, likewise, gained the large support of these oppressed people. His attempts in Mahad town (1927), asserting the right of the untouchables to take water from a public tank, was a crucial event in his career: it integrated the dalits into a formidable group that questioning age-old superstitions and customs shook the foundations of the Hindu society. He successfully organised the labourers and the working classes into a political force demanding freedom from exploitation by landlords, factory-owners and the government. Ambedkar, unlike King, was so placed in history that his country was emerging as a modern nation in its own right at the same time when he was launching his crusade against upper caste oppression. So, he could directly contribute to his country's political evolution: he did this by taking on the responsibility of creating a Constitution for the Indian republic in his capacity as Chairman of the Constitution Drafting Committee.

To understand the importance of the struggle waged by Martin Luther King and B.R. Ambedkar, one needs to examine the condition of the downtrodden at their time in their respective societies and their efforts against great opposition to make a respectable place for their communities in the social milieu. Both the leaders were aware that in spite of the developments over the years, their communities remained economically dependent (with the 'Emancipation Proclamation' after the civil war in America, the blacks had become physically free but not economically; similarly, British education in India had given rise to a broader outlook among western educated Indians and social reformers and reform movements but the dalits still were economically reliant on the other so-called 'superior' castes). The blacks did not own land. The same was true of the dalits in India. In order to escape the drudgery of plantation life, the southern blacks—mostly share croppers and farm labourers—migrated to northern cities to join the industrial labour force with the hope of making a better living. In Indian villages, the dalits were victimised by the landlords, and brahmins and so they were compelled to leave the villages.

Both King and Ambedkar were of the view that only a mass revolution could bring about a significant transformation in the status of their communities and this necessitated a process or programme where political activity went hand in hand with social reform on a broad scale.

Martin Luther King and the Black Movement

King's programme for the emancipation of the black people of America was a well-thoughtout struggle based on integration of the blacks along with economic uplift for their freedom and equal rights to be achieved through a non-violent movement free from racial prejudice. His committed approach and perseverance to continue his fight against all odds without the slightest hint of personal ambition made him the symbol of the civil rights movement of the blacks in America.

King as a Person

King was a man of tireless energy who with great dignity and determination led his people to achieve equal rights and status in society. Perhaps, the best description of Martin Luther King in this sense is to be found in the words of Benjamin Mays, President of Morehouse College, who, honouring him on the college's 90th anniversary, said:

> You are mature beyond your years, wiser at twenty eight than most men of sixty; more courageous in a righteous struggle than most men preach about and never experience. Significant, indeed, is the fact that you did not seek the leadership in the Montgomery controversy. It was thrust upon you by the people. You did not betray that trust of leadership. You led the people with quiet dignity, Christian grace and determined purpose. While you were away, your colleagues in the battle for freedom were being hounded and arrested like criminals. When it was suggested by legal counsel that you might stay away and escape arrest, I heard you say with my own ears: "I would rather spend ten years in jail than desert the people in the crisis." At that moment, my heart, my mind and my soul stood up erect and saluted you. I knew then that you were called to leadership for just such a time as this. On this our 90th anniversary, your Alma Mater is happy to be the first college or university to honor you this way.

Again quoting Emerson, Benjamin Mays referred to King thus: "How masses of men worry themselves into nameless graves when here and there a great soul forgets himself into immortality. "

M.K. Baruah states that Martin Luther King was a short man below average height. He was well-built with strong shoulders and arms and bearing a surgical mark on his chest left by an operation after he was stabbed in the Harlem department store by a black woman. He had a round face and brown eyes and a small moustache, nicely trimmed. Like Gandhi, he loved to walk. He was a good sportsman who had taken part in most of the sports in his school days. In his youth, he was a good dancer. He loved good food and jokingly said that it was his 'only sin'. Healthy, well-built and energetic, he liked to dress well and wore good clothes in public. He was so particular about cleanliness perhaps because he wanted to disprove the white man's remark that the Negroes were always shabby. He loved outdoors, occasionally going out with his family and friends to the mountains. He was a well-read man. The authors he liked to read were James Weldon Johnson, Richard Wright and Langston Hayes, all of them black writers, among others. He loved a close family togetherness and missed the pleasure of it when his work took him reluctantly away from home. His house was cosy and informal. His naturalness and friendliness was felt by everyone who came into contact with him. He enjoyed conversation and was a big talker himself as well as a good listener, never being in a rush.

He liked people. He was shrewd in spite of all his kindness, and could see the motives of men immediately. It was difficult for the reporters and newspapermen to get close to him. They could joke or philosophise with Thurgood Marshall, Roy Wilkins, James Farmer and other black leaders, but King always remained an impenetrable figure. His face was slightly oriental and it never reflected the tensions with which he always lived. But then, King, the private man, had some qualities that were easy and there was something natural about him. He was an infinitely lively soul, serene and friendly, which qualities were mentioned by his wife, Coretta, in her book, *Life with Martin Luther King, Jr.* She says:

> There was something in his manner that was easy. He was easy to know, very friendly. He made people feel a sense of their own worth by not asserting himself. If you did not know who he was, nothing would distinguish him from anybody else.

King as a Leader

King was the architect of achievement of human rights by blacks in America. Though scores of other leaders—some accommodating, some militant revolutionaries—had long before laid the foundation which paved the way for the blacks' fight towards equality and dignity, and had already set into motion the various trends in intellectual, social and moral consciousness of the black people in America, the genius of King recaptured and mobilised this consciousness among his people and helped them to march from the darkness of despair to a new dawn of freedom. The American leaders who kept the fire of freedom burning in the hearts of millions of black citizens in the mostly white land were not only Negro leaders. There were a few truly liberal white leaders also who were responsible for this moral consciousness. They were Thomas Jefferson, Abraham Lincoln and President Kennedy. Among the black leaders who tried to lead their people towards the path of equality and prosperity were Frederick Douglas, Booker T. Washington, W.E. Du Bois, James Weldon Johnson, Phillip Randolph and Roy Wilkins. Each of them created a new consciousness among the blacks and helped them to generate new hopes. All of them did not use the same approach in their call to mobilise the people. Nor did all of them believe in the non-violent method that King preached. The consciousness that all of them brought to the blacks became a great instrument in King's hand for moral-cum-political upheaval. It would not be wrong to say that had King been born fifty years earlier, he could have hardly achieved what he had achieved in his own time. However one cannot dispute the fact that the plight of the blacks today would have been vastly different and their morale would have remained relatively low had King not led the American blacks at that time.

A leader always has his impact on the people and the people on their leader. They grow together. A leader must have courage and faith. A true leader of men must therefore know when to act and when not to act. King was such a leader. He could see the built-up consciousness and emotional discontent among his people. He followed the current of that consciousness by providing the leadership to arouse a spirit of new hope in their minds. He thus won the venture to carry his people from the dark stairs of despair to the lighted attic of hope and freedom.

The quality of moral leadership that King provided has no parallel in American history. He stands high among all other American statesmen and none of them—black or white—could reach his height of morality, even though a few were close to it. No one surpassed his faith and courage. No one loved the masses more than he did. Few equalled him in their universal struggle for freedom of people everywhere.

M.K. Baruah makes an interesting attempt to compare King and other eminent leaders, particularly black leaders like Fredrick Douglas, Booker T. Washington and W.E. Du Bois. He explains that King's views resembled the thinking of these black leaders in some respects even while differing greatly and significantly in some other matters. Like Douglas, King first of all believed in the universal struggle for the freedom of people everywhere and, where the blacks were concerned, spoke for desegregation as well as proposed reforms. Both advocated moral reasoning in place of militant abolitionism. Though, like Booker Washington, King was free of racial prejudice and personal ambition, King was different from him in voicing a need for immediate integration of the blacks in American society. Both King and Du Bois viewed the black problem as a national problem and were willing to lead a struggle putting everything at stake. However, they were temperamentally different. King did not share Du Bois' dislike for the southern white man: Du Bois believed that the southern whites were enemies of the black people and so, they could not be expected or involved to support the blacks, and their civil rights struggle (see Annexure 8).

Black Power and King's Practice of Non-violence

The cry for 'black power' was made by Stokely Carmichael at Greenwood, Mississippi during the freedom march of 1966 which was crucial in strengthening the civil rights demands of the blacks and projecting them as a united front. M.K. Baruah examines the ways in which the cry for militant 'black power' became popular in the context of the civil rights struggle and how King discouraged such violence and advocated non-violence as the right means. The cry for black power which started as a reaction against the brutal white power of Mississippi, soon began to ring all over America. Gradually it developed into a hypothesis that the blacks could no longer believe that their freedom would come through traditional political processes. The black power advocates believed that the white racists had made existing institutions irrelevant, as the blacks did not have proper representation in them. They believed that the poverty and the powerlessness of the black population of the country would perpetuate if they did not organise their own political organisations to make their legitimate demands, to re-evaluate the ideas of the existing social institutions and suggest changes. According to them, black power had to be understood in the context of the history of the black man's struggle for civil rights; in the role of American legislative policies with regard to segregation; in the economics of race relations and in terms of the stagnant ghetto lives of the blacks. The black power advocates believed in open revolution. They were opposed to King's non-violent struggle in solving racial problems. They wanted to identify themselves with Africa and Asia, where two-thirds of the world's black population lived. They felt that those who were not whites were blacks. Speaking of the goals of black power—as compared to those of white racists, Carmichael said:

> The goal of the racists is to keep black people at the bottom, arbitrarily and dictatorially, as they have done in this country for over three hundred years. The goal of black self-determination and black self-identity—black power—is the full participation in the decision-making processes affecting the lives of the black people.

The contention of the black power advocates was that such participation in the decision-making processes could only come through economic and political power, which even the white Jewish people, a minority group, had and they did not. To them, the integration question in America was an attempt by the northern politician to win black votes by talking in terms of the American dream of equality and brotherhood while their southern counterparts appealed to racism to maintain the status quo of segregation. The advocate of black power contended that segregation in America always created an 'imperialistic problem' for the federal government, particularly in dealing with the new African governments who thought that the American blacks virtually remained in colonial status without total freedom. Speaking of the colonial status of the black people, Eldridge Cleaver, a black power advocate, said, "Black people are a stolen people held in a colonial status on stolen land, and any analysis which does not acknowledge the colonial status of black people cannot hope to deal with real problems."

Black people in the United States had always been deprived of land. Elijah Muhammad, a black nationalist, was the first black leader who realised this and said: "We must have our own land, some land of our own, or else." Elijah Muhammad claimed a few states of the United States entirely for the black people, but as he was a black Muslim, his influence on the majority of the blacks was negligible. However, Students Non-Violent Coordinating Committee (SNCC) had tremendous influence on the student community. Majority of SNCC members refused to accept the philosophy of non-violence. Much of the SNCC's criticism was directed against King's non-violent method. Both the SNCC and King's SCLC worked hand in hand. Both stood shoulder-to-shoulder in the Birmingham demonstration of 1963 which was instrumental in the writing of the Civil Rights Act of 1964. Since then the SNCC had been questioning the value of quick scattered demonstrations. They were advocating immediate efforts within the community to educate and organise the southern blacks. SNCC's members were dedicated workers, but they were arrogant. Consciously or unconsciously they borrowed from the thinking of Jean-Paul Sartre. They thought each community must reach its own individual solution. They had a youthful resistance to authority, whether that authority be the white power structure or King's SCLC. Anyone who would fight for freedom was welcomed by them. The SNCC never barred communists and was never contemptuous of anybody who denounced them. The black power advocate insisted on racial separation instead of racial harmony, which King tried to vehemently preach. Its loud cry for racial separation dismayed King to a great extent. The SNCC's advocacy for 'black power' also created many problems for King. These militant students honoured King, but they refused to accept his leadership. They did not think King was radical enough for them. They looked to Stokely Carmichael and other militant student leaders for inspiration. Most of the moderate civil rights groups of black leaders were extremely critical of the black power advocate. However, King did not share the anger of the moderate civil rights leaders. He thought that the inaction of the white power structure and the accommodating nature of the moderate civil rights groups were mainly responsible for the despair and hostility of the younger generation. His wise and understanding heart went to the black power advocate in sympathy. He could very well understand that in their despair, the students had invented the phrase 'black power' as a means of retaliation against the white power structure. He could understand the growing disappointment among these young blacks at the murder of many civil rights workers and the destruction of the black churches by the white racists. To him, the gap that existed between the promises of the white power structure and the fulfilment of those promises, was the cause of the black people's despair. The conditions of the ghettoes in the north, the inhuman discrimination in housing, unemployment, low wages, and the miserable economic plight of the blacks—all these had generated a frustration among the students. These students could not understand how the United States government was fighting for the freedom of the Vietnamese people in South-East Asia some 10,000 miles away when the black people at home were yet to achieve full civil rights. Like Abraham Lincoln, King also considered the evils of racial prejudice as a demon. In 1858, more than 100 years ago, speaking to a group of white men in Illinois, Lincoln had said:

> When you have succeeded in dehumanising the Negroes, when you have put him down and made it impossible for him to be but a beast of the field, when you have extinguished his soul in this world and placed him where the ray of hope is blown out as in the darkness of the damned, are you quite sure that the demon you have aroused will not turn to you?

The demon, of course, was aroused, not only in the mind of the black power advocate but also in the mind of King as well as the last ray of hope to improve the plight of the blacks began to disappear because of the inaction of the white power structure and the federal government. But, the demon that was aroused in King's mind was not clouded by the thought of violence like that of the black power advocate; instead, it helped him to release a new force of non-violence—a soul power, a power which enabled Mahatma Gandhi to crush the power of the mighty British empire. King did not preach violence like the black power advocate but, on the other hand, he tried to bring creative tension in the community.

King is recognised as the first leader from the West to have waged a struggle on the principle of non-violence. When Stokely Carmichael and his followers were advocating violence leading to chaos in the community and were declaring open war against white America, King was preaching non-violence to bring permanent peace to the community. King was openly at war with the white power structure. He wanted to redress the grievances of the poor blacks, exploited by centuries of slavery. He also believed that the blacks should have more economic power, but he differed with the black militant groups in their means to acquire such power. To the black power advocate, end justified the means. King's means were the weapon of love and moral persuasions as against the weapon of violence. While the goal of the black power advocates was to uplift the plight of the blacks alone, King sought, within the goal of the black people, the common goal for all Americans. King did not condemn the idea of black power, but what he condemned was the means that its members used to achieve such power. He even did not approve of the semantics of 'black power', for the slogan 'black power' was likely to be confused with violence which, in turn, would create confusion in the white community. According to him, the use of the semantics of 'black consciousness' or 'black equality' would have been more helpful in advancing the cause of the blacks. He thought that no goodwill and cooperation would be forthcoming from the white people by simply shouting the slogan of 'black power'.

King suggested to the militant groups to follow other constructive means to achieve such power. King's concept of 'black power' was to achieve economic and political power, without resorting to any violence. He thought that "centuries of voicelessness and powerlessness of the Negroes, either in the rural south or in the northern cities, made the Negroes impotent and unable to decide their own destiny." Like other militant groups, King also thought that power was absolutely necessary to do away with the status quo of the black man's life. So, he said:

> The plantation and ghetto were created by those who had power both to confine those who had no power and to perpetuate their powerlessness. The problem of transforming ghetto is, therefore, a problem of power—a confrontation between forces of power demanding change and the forces of power dedicated to preserving the status quo.

Like other militant groups, King also demanded a confrontation with the power that wanted to maintain the status quo. Only, he advocated different means to achieve such power. King believed that only by a moral force, generated from love and goodwill and devoid of hate and abuse, could such a power be acquired. To him, such a power should be desired only to create—not to destroy. He thought that there was nothing wrong if the black people wanted to have power, as long as its attainment was within the range of love, conscience and morality. He was opposed to all arrogance, supremacy, and violence which are generally used to achieve such power.

To King, any power achieved by using violence was always devoid of conscience and as such it was destructive. He urged his people not to abuse power like the white racists. "Such abuse of power," according to King, "is exactly what the Negroes should abhor in the white racists." King admitted that power is always necessary to bring about social, political, and economic changes of a group, but he stressed that it must be accompanied by love and justice.

In this sense, power is not only desirable but necessary in order to implement the demands of love and justice. What is needed is a realisation that power without love is reckless and abusive and love without power is sentimental and anaemic. Power at its best is love implementing the demands of justice. Justice at its best is love correcting everything that stands against love.

With such power of love, King wanted to achieve peaceful revolution in America and to gain power for the black Americans. He warned the militant black power advocate that any revolution born out of despair and violence could not really be successful. It would only perpetuate hatred and would cause destruction. However, as a non-violent leader, King himself did not believe in passivity. He thought that mere passivity was only a sign of cowardice. King did not believe in violent rebellion, nor did he rely on persuasion to achieve freedom and equality for the Negroes; instead, he followed the third course in order to open the eyes of the southern whites to the truth. This he did by advocating Jesus' love as a moral force and Gandhi's *satyagraha* or non-violence, as tactics. For this, King had also to face criticism from the black militant groups in the same way that Washington had to face criticism from Du Bois and the Niagara movement groups. But King was an optimist by way of his faith in the divine just as Washington had been an optimist by deliberate choice.

Again and again, King stressed that a revolution based on non-violence, love and hope only could bring a successful change in society. He urged the black Americans to follow the non-violent methods of Gandhi to achieve their goals. To King, non-violence itself was a power, capable of creating a new society based on love and justice. Non-violence was a moral power. It could eliminate the racial fear from the whites and psychological fear from the blacks; for the latter, fear from their own image—an ugly image created out of several centuries of slave-master relationship. King urged the black political forces to unite and to compel the white majority to listen to the demands of the black citizens. He asked them to pull together their economic resources so that the blacks can emerge as an economic power. He asked them to take pride in their racial heritage and to develop a sense of self-esteem. By doing so, King believed, the blacks could "transform all their scattered forces to a positive and creative power". He pointed out to his people that violence always breeds violence, that it cannot kill prejudices and hatred but can only help in increasing them. He insisted that in order to eradicate all hates and prejudices, one must love and use soul force which has a spiritual power. So, he said:

> Darkness cannot drive out darkness; only light can do that.
> Hate cannot drive out hate, only love can do that.

King thought it would be wrong for the blacks to resort to militant philosophy as demanded by the black power advocates. Some of the leaders of the black power movement declared themselves as defenders of aggressive violence, but to King "the line of demarcation between defensive violence and aggressive violence" was a very narrow one. King abhorred all kinds of violence for they could only bring chaos and confusion to a society. He felt the methods to gain power advocated by the black power group, were not effective. To him, it was only an "expression of weakness—not of strength." He also rejected the loud cry of the militant group that the black people constitute the majority of the world population; hence they should not be afraid to unite together to gain power for all the black people of the world. "Those who are not white are black" was their view. King wanted to point out to the militant groups that people in Asia and Africa were busy fighting their own battles against poverty. They did not have time to think about gaining united power for all black people. King advised the black militants that instead of trying for revolution of the black people throughout the world through violence, they should take the lead to help the poor people of Asia and Africa to alleviate their poverty, so that the "hope of all the coloured people of the world may be realised through the American Negroes".

King was pragmatic. He thought that it was unrealistic for the blacks to follow a separate road of power for the fulfilment of their goals. He also thought that there could not be any "salvation of Negroes through isolation". King considered black separatism to be as morally unsound as white racism. According to him, in a multiracial society like the United States, no group could exist on its own since all groups were inter-dependent. King also rejected the black power advocate's notion that white America cannot look after the black interest. Citing examples of many dedicated whites who were working for civil rights movements, King said that it would be a mistake for the blacks to reject everything American and look towards Africa. To him, the American black was a hybrid of Africa and the West. He was an Afro-American. The American black was an integral part of the American society; he had helped to build America with labour, sweat and pain so it would be a mistake to seek a separate black society. He said that the blacks could improve the society by "finding ... security and justice within the country". To King, total freedom could be achieved by the blacks only by sharing power with other power groups. He said that "liberation cannot come without integration, integration cannot come without liberation". He believed that it was only by "mutual sharing of power" by the black and white citizens that the conditions of housing, education, and health of the black people could be improved. He thought that by following a separate road to power, the blacks would never be able to improve their condition as they do not have the resources. On the other hand, King advocated power for the poor people of all ethnic groups. He thought that mutual sharing of power would bring racial harmony in America. He believed that the American blacks should play a "dynamic role in revolutionising the entire nation" to solve the racial problems and poverty in the country and thereby leading all

Americans irrespective of colour, creed and race to a desired standard of human dignity and decency in that affluent society.

To King, black power, as advocated by the militant, was "radical and uncompromising". King believed, as Gandhi did, that there are times when a good cause can be helped by working with the authority, even though the authority is bad. While the militant black power advocate only criticised the existing white institution, King wanted to present the injury and injustices suffered by the blacks at the hands of the ruling white power structure in such a way that it could arouse more sorrow than hatred. It could appeal more to the conscience of the white people. King wanted to fight the cause of animosity and distrust rather than encourage it. The militant black power advocate wanted only to paint a darker picture of the existing society of that time in such a way that it would destroy all the values of the society.

To trace the career of King as a champion of the blacks' cause to achieve civil rights and a status equal as that of the whites in society, we have to begin at the first important incident of his career which not only vaulted him into national prominence but also saw remarkable co-operation among the blacks to stand united in a steadfast struggle for gaining what was their due and ending all discrimination against them. This incident was the historical Montgomery bus boycott of 1955 that laid the foundation of King's civil rights struggle. In his book, *Strides Toward Freedom* (1958), he narrates the factors and events that led to his call for the bus boycott by the blacks in Montgomery and describes how and why the event succeeded as a peaceful resistance against the established (white) authority and in uniting the blacks as never before. He recounts his fears and expectations as the incident unfolded itself and the deliberation and resolutions undertaken to keep the protest going. King speaks of how the bus boycott events gave the black community a new strength to struggle and instilled in them a sense of dignity and destiny (see Annexure 9).

The Washington March of 1963

The Washington March to demand racial equality was an important as well as historical march which is considered as one of three important marches in the world. These three are the one started by chairman Mao, the march in Washington in 1963 of which King was one of the main organisers and the third historical Namantran March by Prof. Kawade. King, who was, by this time, already a prominent leader of the blacks' civil rights struggle, won further acclaim with the success of the Washington March.

The great march in Washington on August 28, 1963, also called the long march, was more than a demonstration to demand jobs and freedom. It also tried to free all Americans from racial bias and fear. It was a dignified demonstration of twenty million blacks to obtain their human rights.

The purpose of the march was to register protests against discrimination in housing and employment, and the alleged discrimination in the ranks of the federal government particularly by the Department of Justice.

The final plan for the march was drafted in New York at a meeting of various civil rights groups, including the National Association for the Advancement of Colored People, (NAACP), Congress of Racial Equality (CORE), SNCC, Negro American Labour Council, SCLC and the National Council of Negro Women. They all formed a united front to conduct the proposed march. All these black organisations also decided to stage this march in Washington as the attention of the senators and members of the Congress could easily be drawn there.

On August 24, 1963, marchers began to arrive in the city of Washington from all over America. Slowly the demonstrators swirled around the monuments and the assembly grounds. At the monuments folk singers rendered their songs and others sang civil rights songs. The demonstrators then began to march from the Washington monuments to the Lincoln Memorial. Some wept as they marched. It was an orderly crowd, with a clear sense of common endeavour to reach a fixed destination.

Finally, the formal programme began. Speaker after speaker appeared on the platform. Many leaders made their speeches. Famous black singer Mahalia Jackson stepped on the platform and sang the sorrowful gospel song titled, "I have been bucked and I have been scorned". The song moved her audience to tears. After Miss Jackson left the platform, King began to speak about the plight of the blacks after hundred years of emancipation:

> But one hundred years later, we must face the tragic fact that the Negro is still not free. One hundred years later, the life of the Negro is still sadly crippled by the manacles of segregation and the chains of discrimination. One hundred years later, the Negro lives on a lonely island of poverty in the midst of a vast ocean of material prosperity. One hundred years later, the Negro is still languishing in the corners of American society and finds himself an exile in his own land.

King declared that the Negroes would not be satisfied "until justice rolls down like waters and righteousness like a mighty stream". King's speech reached its height when he began to speak with some phrases, smooth and connected without any break between the successive sentences. It brought repeated cheers from the massive crowd like rolling waves when they touch the mighty seashore. The crowd was again warmed up by then. They began to interrupt the speech with tremendous applause as King described his great American dream:

> I have a dream today. I have a dream that one day in the red hills of Georgia the sons of former slaves and sons of former slave owners will be able to sit down together at the table of brotherhood.
>
> I have a dream that one day even the state of Mississippi, a desert state sweltering with the heat of injustice and

oppression, will be transformed into an oasis of freedom and justice.

I have a dream that my four little children will one day live in a nation where they will not be judged by the colour of their skin but by the content of their character.

I have a dream today.

I have a dream that one day the state of Alabama, whose governor's lips are presently dripping with the words of interposition and nullification, will be transformed into a situation where little black boys and black girls will be able to join hands with little white boys and white girls and walk together as sisters and brothers.

I have a dream today.

I have a dream that one day every valley shall be exalted, every hill and mountain shall be made low, the rough places will be made plains, and the crooked places will be made straight, and the glory of the Lord shall be revealed, and all flesh shall see it together.

This is our hope. This is the faith with which I return to the south. With this faith we will be able to hew out of the mountain of despair a stone of hope. With this faith we will be able to transform the jangling discords of our nation into a beautiful symphony of brotherhood. With this faith we will be able to work together, to struggle together, to go to jail together, to stand up for freedom together, knowing that we will be free one day.

This will be the day when all of God's children will be able to sing with new meaning "My country is of thee, sweet land of liberty, of thee I sing. Land where my fathers died, land of the pilgrim's pride, from every mountainside, let freedom ring!"

And if America is to be a great nation this must become true. So let freedom ring from the prodigious hilltops of New

> Hampshire! Let freedom ring from the mighty mountains of New York! Let freedom ring from the heightening Alleghenies of Pennsylvania!
>
> Let freedom ring from the snowcapped Rockie of Colorado!
>
> Let freedom ring from the curvaceous peaks of California!
>
> But only that, let freedom ring from Stone Mountain of Georgia!
>
> Let freedom ring from every hill and mole hill of Mississippi. From every mountainside, let freedom ring.
>
> When we let freedom ring, when we let it ring from every village and every hamlet, from every state and every city, we will be able to speed up that day when all of God's children, black and white men, Jews and Gentiles, Protestants and Catholics, will be able to join hands and sing in the words of that old Negro spiritual, "Free at last! Free at last! Thank God almighty, we are free at last!"

After King finished, there were some final ceremonies, but all the effective interest and purpose of the day was over. The marchers then began to leave the city. It was a quiet night in Washington after such an eventful day which shall never be forgotten.

King restated his dream from the blue print of the Declaration of Independence.

His speech had the impact of the ages. Like Abraham Lincoln's famous speech at Gettysburg, or like President Kennedy's inaugural speech of 1961, King's speech will be remembered forever. Almost all of the newspapers editorialised it as one of the remarkable ideas. King's speech was conciliatory and balanced. Someone charged that he had compromised with the whites, but there was no diplomacy involved in the speech. There was no tone of accommodation or compromise.

The black people made some civil rights gains after the passage of civil rights bills in 1964. But federal laws met racist resistance in many places of the south during their enforcement. Such resistance occasionally led to violence.

The Freedom March of 1966

Once again King played a crucial role and was successful in making the march a non-violent one. This march is also significant as the cry for 'black power' originated here.

The southern blacks became panicky at these racist atrocities. James Meredith, a civil right worker, decided to march alone to dramatise the racial situation in Mississippi and to get fear out of the minds of the Mississippi blacks. When Meredith was marching in June 1966, he was shot in his back on Highway 51. King, who was busy with his Chicago movement at that time, went to Mississippi to see things and to express sympathy to Meredith who luckily survived. At the same time, Floyd McKissic, then director of CORE, also went to Mississippi to express sympathy to Meredith. After conferring with Meredith, King and McKissic decided to continue Meredith's unfinished march in order to demonstrate that the blacks would not be intimidated by the terror of violence perpetrated by the white extremists. Later on Stokely Carmichael, the president of SNNC, also joined them at the hospital. After a brief discussion, all of them agreed to sponsor jointly the unfinished march of Meredith. It was agreed to invite other civil rights organisations to join them.

Thus, the second stage of the Freedom March began from the spot on Highway 51 where Meredith discontinued it after he was shot. The march proceeded peacefully for the first few days. There were occasional resentments among the black students, mostly among SNCC members against the inclusion of some white marchers. Some of these students questioned the usefulness of King's non-violent method if the unarmed marchers were attacked on highways. King urged them not to have such an attitude. He tried to reason with the SNCC members, who were mostly students. He tried to make the students understand that the blacks and whites must work together to create an environment of racial understanding in order to arouse the conscience of the whole nation. King also pointed out to the students that there were dedicated white men who had worked hard for racial justice and had sacrificed their lives. He tried to impress on them that it would be a mistake to exclude and repudiate dedicated men and women. So King insisted on the inclusion of the white marcher and urged all of them to make the march a non-violent one. Finally everyone agreed to King's proposal.

The march continued. They marched for ten days on the highway and reached Greenwood county. The SNCC members had worked in that county in the summer of 1964 and and had established their influence, reputation, and goodwill among the inhabitants. The SNCC was a broad federation of the southern youth, mainly, though not exclusively, black. It had electrified the whole nation with sit-in demonstrations in 1960–61. While the marchers were marching to Greenwood, a mass meeting was held in the city park. Many march leaders including King spoke at that meeting. Stokely Carmichael, the then SNCC president, emphasised in the speech, the need for 'black power'. Another SNCC leader Willie Ricks, perhaps as planned earlier, immediately got up to the platform and asked the audience, "What do you want?" The SNCC students replied, "black power". For the second time Ricks asked, "What do you want?" and the crowd shouted louder, "black power, black power". Thus was born the cry of 'black power' which came to be associated with the militant outlook.

The Assassination Attempt on King

M.K. Baruah describes in detail the incident of the assassination attempt on King by 42-year old Izola Curry who was finally committed to the Nathewan state hospital for the criminally insane. He discusses the reactions the incident generated in the black community and among the black leaders (see Annexure 10).

In 1968, King was assassinated in Memphis, Tennessee by one James Earl Ray who was later convicted of the murder though there was little evidence to suggest that he had committed the crime. King was only thirty-nine years old when he died yet he was six years older than Thomas Jefferson, who died at the age of thirty-three, and two years younger than the age at which Abraham Lincoln, who took office a hundred years before him, and John F. Kennedy, the youngest president of the United States, died. These were men who had zest for life, whose political actions evolved from their spiritual belief, and who sought the broadest possible self-realisation. King was such a man. What made King one of the greatest figures of the Western world? If anyone examines his life very closely, he will find that it was his untiring search for the truth that all men are created equal by the God, and his self-realisation of such a truth that made him one of the greatest personalities of the twentieth century. Benjamin Mays, eulogising King, said,

> It does not matter how long he lived, but people will always judge how well he did. Future history will judge King by his deeds.

The impact of his great unfinished task to achieve equality for the black Americans had been enormous. He pursued a course of social progress not only for his own people but also for all Americans. His philosophy of social justice and advancement of the poor people perhaps can be best described by President Kennedy's famous statement, "If a free society cannot help the many who are poor, it cannot save the few who are rich."

King was the voice and the instrument of the second American revolution, the organiser of unity among his fellow Negroes, the abolitionist of the Jim Crow law on public conveyances in the south and the advocate of non-violence and brotherhood for a divided people. For a while his work turned the black ghettos of America into battlegrounds. The whole world and the nation managed to bear King's loss. But it was particularly a great loss for the black people who had found a new hope under his leadership and had won a great battle against injustice through non-violence—a struggle that attracted the admiration of the world.

The immediate effect of the assassination of King was that it sparked off a black rampage that subjected America to one of the most widespread spasms of racial disorder in its history. The fire that started in Washington created a scene beyond imagination. Helmeted troops, bayoneted rifles guarding the White House and light machine guns posted at the steps of the Capitol Hill, made it look like it was on fire. The national guard was called on duty in many cities. Curfew was enforced.

King's death brought some black students closer to the leadership of Stokely Carmichael and to the philosophy of black nationalism. These students mostly accepted King's philosophy of non-violence but after King's death non-violence as a tactic ceased to be effective to a certain extent as there was no other black leader in America at that time who could on the basis of non-violence or even otherwise give effective leadership to his community, mobilising the various forces reflecting the desire and aspirations of the black citizens. So, after King's death, a vacuum was created within the black leadership.

Increasing pressure in the first half of the 1960s had already led to the passage of federal legislation, the Civil Rights Act of 1964 and the Voting Rights Act of 1965 under President Lyndon Johnson. The United States Congress passed a civil rights housing bill immediately after King's death. Some hailed that as an honour to King, but the racist law-makers from the south who opposed the bill condemned it as an act of cowardice legislature. Even after the passing of many civil rights, the racial problems in the United States could not be solved immediately as there was no apparent improvement in the race relations between the blacks and the whites.

King had dreamt of an America where every citizen would have equal rights and where there would not be inequalities in distribution of wealth, and where a person would not be judged by the colour of his skin but by his true worth as an individual. But like Christ, he had become a victim of the same force: the violence of extremists. In 1985, Congress enacted a law to commemorate the birth date of King. He is the only American to have a national holiday in his honour.

In many parts of India, the death of King was mourned. King as a leader has great significance from the Indian viewpoint not only owing to his advocating Gandhi's non-violence but also because of his striking resemblance to Ambedkar. The Indian parliament paid homage to King. On his death, Indira Gandhi, the then Prime Minister of India, described King as "an apostle of peace, one of mankind's finest products, and a great evangelist of equality of man".

In his journey from the beginning at Montgomery to the end at Memphis, Martin Luther King, Jr. found time, amid a career of social activism, to write sermons and essays. His important sermons are collected in *Strength to Love* (1963), *A Martin Luther King Treasury* (1964) and *Trumpet of Conscience* (1967). Similarly, his major essays are collected in *Why We Can't Wait* (1964) and *Where Do We Go from Here: Chaos or Community*? (1967).

Inevitably, many biographers have attempted to chart the life and career of Martin Luther King, Jr. Three biographers appeared during his lifetime: Lawrence Reddick, *Crusader Without Violence* (1959); Edward T. Clayton, *Martin Luther King, Jr.: The Peaceful Warrior* (1964); and Lerone Bennett, Jr., *What Manner of Man* (1965). Following his untimely death in April 1968, a grief-stricken world showered his memory with eulogising tributes and several biographies. Some of the more important works are Robert M. Bleiweiss, *Marching to Freedom*

(1968); G. Gerasimov, *Fire Bell in the Night* (translated from the Russian in 1968); William R. Miller, *Martin Luther King, Jr.: His Life, Martyrdom, and Meeting for the World* (1968); Coretta Scott King, *My Life With Martin Luther King, Jr.* (1969); and David L. Lewis, *King: A Critical Biography* (1970).

Nobel Prize and King

King was awarded the Nobel Peace Prize in 1964. Gunnar John, chairman of the Norwegian Parliament's Noble Committee, stated, "Dr. King is the first person in the western world to have shown us that a struggle can be waged without violence." The letter to the Nobel Committee recommending King for the award said that since 1955, "Dr. King has emerged as the most important Negro leader in the U.S., devoted to non-violence and peaceful struggle, and was setting an example for the colored people all over the world."

But the 1964 Nobel Peace Prize award became a very controversial issue in America. There were people who questioned whether the Nobel Peace Prize, the award for the international peacemaker of the year, should go to a man whose fame was based upon his battle for civil rights for the black Americans and whose activities often led to violence. Again, there were people who admired the decision-makers for such a wise selection for the Nobel award. Most people and newspapers in the north welcomed the news, while the same news came as a surprise to many southern whites. An elderly woman wrote to the editor of a southern newspaper questioning the Nobel Peace Committee's decision in awarding the peace prize to King, whose protest marches so often resulted in sporadic violence.

The first black leader to receive the Nobel Peace Prize had been Robert Luthuli, the South African black leader, in 1960. The second had been Ralph Bunche, an American black leader. King was the third black leader to receive it. On hearing the news, King issued from the hospital the following statement: "I do not consider this merely an honor to me personally, but a tribute to the disciplined, wisely restrained and majestic courage of the millions of gallant Negro and white persons of goodwill who have followed a non-violent course in seeking to establish a reign of justice and a rule of love across this nation of ours."

This was the second time in the history of Atlanta that a black citizen had been so honoured. The first was Booker T. Washington who delivered his famous Atlanta compromise speech at the Cotton States International Exposition in 1893. The white citizens honoured him because Washington assured the city that the blacks under his leadership would perfect their manual talents and would not claim any political, cultural or social equality with the whites. But the celebration honouring King was a different occasion. It was quite the opposite of Washington's promise which King made to the white citizens on that night. King promised to lead his fellow Negroes to the just ladder of equality and to free them from the economic exploitation by the white power structure.

On that night, the whites of Atlanta honoured him despite his forthright declaration that he would neither equivocate nor compromise but lead the blacks to achieve total freedom in all areas of life.

Ambedkar and Emancipation of the Dalits

Like King, Ambedkar's commitment to work for the downtrodden in his society was marked by determination at the outset and by perseverance throughout his career. He was able to generate a new consciousness, a remarkable sense of 'awakening' among the dalits and they came to rely on him as a leader to be completely trusted and followed. He dedicated his life to the struggle for liberation of the dalits from centuries of slavery and this earned him respect from millions in India and abroad.

Ambedkar, like King, was a man of strict discipline, good habits and fine moral calibre. Just as King, Ambedkar was a dreamer; he dreamt of social change that would inspire a new dawn of equality among castes on the Indian soil, an equality that would gain recognition for all time to come. In a ringing tone, Ambedkar declared that it was not enough to do away with untouchability leaving the system of caste alone. He advocated inter-dining and inter-marriage among Hindus of various castes to get rid of the caste system itself.

When we study the career of Ambedkar, we find that Ambedkar was deeply involved in efforts to improve the condition of the dalits even before he had stepped into his thirties.

Ambedkar started his mission from 1919 onwards. In order to bring socio-political awakening to the depressed classes he started *Mook Naik* (Leader of the Dumb), a fortnightly in Marathi from Bombay on January 31, 1920. For the emancipation of the depressed classes, he formed the Bashishkrit Hitkarini Sabha (Depressed Classes Welfare Organisation) on July 20, 1924 at Bombay. The Sabha started one hostel at Sholapur for high school students belonging to the dalits. Later on, he founded the Depressed Classes Education Society on June 14, 1928.

Mahad March (1927)

The Chowdar tank situated in the Mahad town in the Colaba district of Bombay Presidency was handed over to the Mahad municipality when the same was established in 1869. This tank which was the main source of water for the inhabitants of Mahad town was not to be used by the dalits. The only source of water for the untouchable was the well and scattered dirty water in the town. The well was at some distance from the centre of the town. This created great hardship for dalits in getting proper water.

In 1923, the Legislative Council of Bombay passed a resolution to the effect that the untouchable classes be allowed to use public wells and dharmshalas which are built and maintained out of the public funds or administered by bodies appointed or created by statutes as well as public schools, courts, offices and dispensaries. In pursuance of the above resolution, the government issued orders and the Mahad municipality also passed a resolution in 1924 to the effect that the municipality had no objection to allow the untouchables to use the Chowdar tank. But, the caste-Hindus in Mahad were not happy and were hostile on this score.

It was then that Ambedkar organised the untouchables to assert their legal right to take water from the tank.

At Mahad, a conference of dalits on March 19 and 20, 1927 was attended by about 10,000 delegates. Untouchables from all over the country attended the conference at Mahad called by Ambedkar to consider their plight. At this conference, they took a historic decision to burn the Hindu book of laws called the *Manusmriti*, which had kept them in slavery for thousands of years. They also declared their resolve to take water from public water-tanks, from which they had been prohibited by law, and set a date to enter the Kala Ram temple at Nasik from which they were also prohibited.

Addressing this conference, Ambedkar said:

> We are not condemned by any god, nor is it because of our deeds in our past birth that we were driven to this sorry state. We are untouchables because it benefited others. What we have lost others have gained. Our humiliation has been a matter of pride for others.

He pointed to the cause of their troubles, the *Manusmriti*, which he ceremoniously burned at this conference as an open act of defiance. Then he led the march to the public tank from where they all took water. He declared "If we are Hindus, then we must enter Hindu temples." He led the procession to Kala

Ram Mandir at Nasik—but before they reached it, Hindus closed the temple and put sentries round the holy ground.

These provocative actions shook the foundation of Hindu society: such actions had previously been unheared of. When asked, Ambedkar said:

> We did not drink water from the public tank because we were dying without, nor did we want to worship in temples for personal salvation. We performed the actions because it is our right as free human beings.

The motives behind Ambedkar's actions were clear-cut. He wanted the untouchables themselves to be aware of their situation and said:

> Discard the thought that any god or superman is going to do anything for you. Have firm faith in your goals because nobody else is going to break your age-old shackles of slavery. Remember, goats are sacrificed but never lions.

He was preparing them for a greater struggle to come. He also threw his gauntlet before Hindu society and declared: "Enough is enough." The time had come when they would not tolerate any of the atrocities which had become a pastime for the so-called higher castes.

Ambedkar belonged to the working people of India, the dalits. The pains and the miseries of the workers and the peasants who comprised the dalits were his own. He identified himself with the masses and the classes in their trials and tribulations. He took a keen interest in abolishing the khoti and watan system of land relations in order to prevent peasants' exploitation. His contribution to the uplift of the dalits in India has to be seen in terms of his concern for the working class of India and his efforts to organise the working class movement.

The Labour Movement

Ambedkar put forth the principle of 'social equality' as the major ideological offensive against Hindu orthodoxy. The

'Social Equality League' by Ambedkar and his friends stood for application of the principle of equality in all fields—religious, social, political and economic. His commitment to the essential equality of human beings was total.

He upheld the workers' democratic right to strike. But he opposed the Bombay textile strike led by the Girni Kamgar Union in April 1929, owing to the hypocrisy of the communist leaders who had never raised their voice against the prohibitive barriers that kept the depressed class workers away from the lucrative departments of the mill industry. The untouchables were not allowed in the weaving sections, lest they pollute the thread and others who touch it. Similar discrimination and practice of untouchability prevailed in the railways too. Moreover, unemployment and debt burden was more heavy on the depressed class workers. Ambedkar's opposition to the strike which was based on 'economism'[1] was fully justified by subsequent revelations about the character of the leadership.[2]

The depressed classes were not a political force in any form before 1936. According to the Government of India Act of 1935, general elections were to take place in 1937. The Indian National Congress was one of the biggest parties having a following in every province. There were other parties also like the Muslim League, but the dalits had no political party of their own. At this critical time Ambedkar took the lead and formed the Independent Labour Party in August 1936.

The party fought the general elections in the Old Bombay Presidency. Out of the 15 seats assigned to the scheduled classes in Bombay Presidency, it captured 13 and, in addition, it won two general seats. Ambedkar fought his election in Bombay and was elected. This was the first victory for the dalits.

Labour Party

The party had a programme for the workers and the peasants as well as the lower middle classes. It favoured legislation to protect tenants from exactions and evictions by the landlords as also for certain benefits as available to industrial workers. The programme envisaged rehabilitation of old industries, starting new ones and the principle of state management and state ownership of industries wherever necessary. For raising the productivity and efficiency of the people, an extensive programme of technical education was put forth. In the industrial sector, legislation to control employment and conditions of service and work was proposed. The party had a clear-cut programme for land settlement and starting of public works aimed at addressing the unemployment problem. It campaigned for house rent control in industrial centres and big towns in the interest of the lower middle class. It also had a definite social programme against all forms of orthodoxy and reaction and suggested use of charity funds for secular purposes like education. Village planning for sanitation, housing and modernisation with cultural facilities was also projected.

Explaining the rationale behind the new party of the working people, Ambedkar pointed out that the Congress was a combination of the exploiters and the exploited and it was not useful for the purpose of social reconstruction. He said that the Congress was ruled by the capitalists and that as long as their control continued there was no scope for betterment of the economic condition of the depressed classes. Therefore, he called for a united front against the capitalists to win economic independence and declared that the working people had nothing to lose and had everything to gain by this.

Ambedkar organised massive peasant rallies in different parts of Bombay Province and led a big march to the Council Hall in Bombay in early 1938. The processionists carried posters bearing slogans such as "Down with the Khoti System" and "Support Dr. Ambedkar's Bill".[3] They demanded enforcement of minimum standard of wages for agricultural labourers and remittances of rent as also revenue arrears. Apart from legislation for abolition of khoti system and inamdar system, they demanded reduction of fifty per cent of irrigation rates payable by small holders. Addressing a mammoth meeting of the peasants and workers at the Esplanade Maidan, Ambedkar observed that "there are two classes in the world—the haves and the havenots, the rich and the poor, the exploiters and the exploited". He, therefore, exhorted the peasants and workers to think about the causes of their poverty which lay in the richness of the exploiters. The way out for them was to organise a labour front without any regard to caste or creed; this would ensure shelter, clothing and food for the producers.[4]

Ambedkar paid special attention to the problems of the railway workers. A big conference of untouchable railway workers was convened at Manmad in February 1938. He criticised the communist trade union leaders for not taking up the question of untouchability and social injustice as they feared a split among the workers. He was very clear about the enemies of the working class in India: they were Brahminism and capitalism. About Brahminism, he stated:

> By Brahminism I do not mean the power, privileges and interests of the Brahmins as a community. That is not the sense in which I am using the word. By Brahminism I mean the negation of the spirit of liberty, equality and fraternity. In that sense, it is rampant in all classes and is not confined to Brahmins alone though they have been its originators. The effects of Brahminism were not confined only to social rights such as inter-dining and inter-marrying. It denied them also the civic rights. So omniscient is Brahminism that it even affects the field of economic opportunities.[5]

He observed that there were many appointments from which a depressed class worker was kept out by reason of his being an untouchable, as in the textile industry. In the railways it was their lot to work as gangmen. They were not even appointed as porters because porters were engaged as domestic servants by the station masters and the depressed class workers, being untouchables, were dropped out. The same conditions prevailed in the railway workshops. He wondered how to consolidate the working classes when such glaring injustice and partiality which worked against the principle of solidarity was prevalent. He felt uprooting of Brahminism necessary to inculcate the spirit of equality among the workers and unite them. He was surprised at M.N. Roy's opposition to the existence of a separate party of labour.[6]

Roy's argument was that destruction of imperialism was the first and foremost aim of Indian politics. But Ambedkar rejected this thesis and put forth the idea that imperialism cannot be fought without fighting the landlords, mill-owners and moneylenders who were in alliance with imperialism. He observed that a communist opposing separate political organisation of labour was a contradiction in terms.[7]

Industrial Disputes Bill of 1938

In the second half of 1938, the Congress government of Bombay introduced the Industrial Disputes Bill which came under stringent criticism from the trade unions. Ambedkar led the attack in the Legislative Assembly. The bill was sought to replace the Bombay Trade Disputes Conciliation Act of 1934 and provided that conciliation shall be compulsory and that strikes under certain circumstances would be illegal. Ambedkar criticised the provision regarding the conciliation procedures which virtually snatched away the workers' right to organise. He held that the provisions which stipulated conviction and imprisonment for 'illegal' strike was bad in law because strike could not be considered a crime and it was only an act of omission and civil wrong for which remedies were to be provided to the aggrieved person who suffered the breach of contract or civil wrong. He referred to the law regarding civil wrong with particular reference to breach of contracts of service and pointed out that the employer was entitled to damages only and the court could never compel a man to perform the contract of service which he has entered upon.

Ambedkar traced the history of Indian law to see how breach of contract of service could be treated as a crime. He pointed out that this interpretation had been first made in the Workmen's Breach of Contract Act of 1857, soon after the mutiny or during the course of it. The express purpose of such a provision had been to compel the artisans who had contracted to provide essential materials for the British army to continue to provide the services during the mutiny. This Act, although a formal statute from 1857, had never been put into operation. It was amended in 1920 with salutary provisions authorising the magistrate to look into the equity of the contract before punishing the recalcitrant workman notwithstanding the fact that he had taken an advance from his employer. The 1920 Act also provided for punishment of an employer who brought a frivolous complaint. The provision of the Indian Penal Code (IPC) also did not cover the breach of contract in the case of ordinary factory workers. They referred to the services of seamen, services to be rendered at a distant place to which the servant was conveyed at the expense of the master and breach of contract on the part of an attendant in supplying the wants of helpless persons. The last item covered in section 491 of the IPC was the only section which was retained and the others were repealed. Thus Ambedkar established that strike which was a forbidding word for a breach of contract of service was not a crime and not punishable under the Indian law. It was only a civil wrong for which the remedy could only be damages and never a specific performance. He emphasised that the Indian law did not name a breach of contract of service a crime, because to make it a crime was to compel a man to serve against his will making him a slave. "To penalise a strike, therefore," Ambedkar contended, "is nothing short of making the worker a slave." Quoting the Constitution of the USA he asserted that slavery was nothing else but involuntary servitude and that the bill which declared strike as a crime was contrary to ethics and contrary to jurisprudence. As regards the right to strike, he maintained that it was simply another name for the right to freedom. It was nothing else than the right to the freedom of one's services on any terms that one wants to obtain. Once the right to freedom is conceded, the right to strike is necessarily conceded. He further contended that "if the right to freedom is a divine right then the right to strike is also a divine right".

Ambedkar dubbed the Industrial Disputes Bill as the Workers Civil Liberties Suspension Act, and said that it would bring about perpetual slavery as it provided that "there shall be no strike at all for one year after the Act comes into operation" and that the workers would have to go through a cumbersome conciliatory procedure extending to four months and 25 days. during which they must do nothing. Such restrictions not only on mobilisation and organisation but even the right to speak was nothing but complete slavery. He referred to a minute of dissent given by Jamna Das Mehta and others on the 1929 bill and pointed out that a strike in a public utility service which should not be considered essential ought not be visited with criminal prosecution. Yet, it was granted that services like water supply, light and sanitation were absolutely essential to the very existence of the society and so any strike in such services should be discouraged by legitimate means not because they are public utility services but because they are social security services.

He argued for the exclusion of public utilities like railways from the definition of essential services. He stressed that the essential services should be only those services essential for public safety and life of the community. He also attacked the provisions regarding conciliation with the representatives of employees. It was provided in the bill that only unions representing more than fifty per cent of the workers and unions having twenty per cent of workers as its members and recognised by the employer were entitled to represent the labour. He pointed out that even in industrialised countries like England the total proportion of unionised workers was much below fifty per cent of the total workforce and the stipulation of fifty per cent membership for recognition as the bargaining agent was unreasonable and arbitrary. Ambedkar also opposed the clause which stipulated that the Registrar shall not register more than one union in any local area in respect of any industry or occupation. This restricted the potential of the union growing on a countrywide basis and the growth of the general labour unions as was the case in England and other western countries.

Ambedkar also exposed the government's claim that the bill sought to treat the employers and employees on equal footing. In this connection he gave a powerful argument to demolish the equality doctrine on the basis of equity. Equality is not necessarily equity. In order that it may produce equity in society, in order that it may produce justice in society, the different people have to be treated unequally. To prove this point, he asked what the basis was for the system of progressive income tax where the rich were taxed at a higher rate and poor at a lower rate because the taxable capacity of the two was different. In such a case equality would produce the greatest inequity. He cited the case of an ordinary household where there are several persons of whom one is sick. In order that the sick person may get better he may be given chicken soup, but others are not given soup. But no one would blame the mother of the household if she gave chicken soup to the sick member and denied it to the other members enjoying robust health. Therefore, equity cannot be achieved if we treat the strong and the weak, the rich and the poor, the ignorant and the intelligent on the same footing. He further urged that the workers' wages should be the first charge on the profit of the industry. He reiterated:

> .... there is no basis for equality between capital and labour because the government in any dispute is always on the side of the employer. This is clear from the use of police the

> government makes in strike. The police force is maintained out of public funds, out of the taxes borne by all and it is intended to benefit all society. And no government is entitled to use the police force merely because a strike by the workers results in breach of peace. Further, if the breach of peace is caused by some unreasonable demand made by labour, the use of police force may be justified. On the contrary, if the breach of peace is due to the employer, due to his unjust, unreasonable and iniquitous stand, then the government has no right to use the police against the workers.

Such a powerful defence of the workers' basic right to decide the terms on which they would work is very rare in the annals of India's working class movement. Ambedkar presented a strong case for a workers' democracy.

When we analyse the ideas of Ambedkar, we find that he was different from Martin Luther King in his approach to the problems of emancipating the dalits. He wanted to see the dalits as militant. An important cause behind this philosophy was that he was the son of an army officer. This was at a time when the dalits were victims of innumerable atrocities. It was in keeping with this spirit that he founded the Samata Sainik Dal in March 1927. Basically it was to enlist support for the Mahad *satyagraha* and maintain discipline during the *satyagraha* and in the society. It was, however, formally organised at a national level on July 20, 1942 at Nagpur. Its first conference was held under the presidentship of Sardar Gopal Singh of Punjab. Ambedkar addressed the conference.

Ambedkar's Contribution to Constitution-Making

Ambedkar was born at a time when India was witnessing one of the crucial periods in its history, a time when it was emerging as an independent modern state. Ambedkar's efforts for socio-political reform and liberty of the downtrodden in society, unlike King's, were placed in the context of a newly-emerging and evolving modern state. The Indian state that grew out of the British colonial empire in South Asia had great dreams and hopes for the future and the spirit to achieve its dreams. Ambedkar was thus placed in a situation where, with his remarkable vision and qualities like perseverance and commitment, he could contribute in diverse ways to the development of his nation. This he did.

One major achievement of Baba Saheb Ambedkar was constitution-making. As the chief architect of the Indian Constitution, he defined its vision. He looked upon democracy as not just a part of government, but a faith which decides one's attitudes to others. He wanted constitutional basis for socialism because the experience of political democracies had shown that the legislatures and governments, even under adult suffrage, were controlled by the more powerful. Therefore, he put forward the proposal for safeguarding the liberty of the individual. "The soul of democracy," observed Ambedkar, "is the doctrine of one man, one value." His aim, therefore, was to avoid the vagaries of dictatorship and to have socialism with parliamentary democracy.

Apart from the proposals on fundamental rights and safeguards against its invasion, the constitutional proposal of Ambedkar included provisions for the protection of the minorities and scheduled castes also.

At the time of the final reading of the Constitution in November 1949, Ambedkar observed:

> On the economic plane, we have a society in which there are some who have immense wealth as against many who live in abject poverty. On 26 January 1950, we are going to enter into a life of contradictions. In politics we will have equality and in social and economic life we will have inequality. In politics we will be recognising the principles of one man, one vote, one value. In our social and economic life, we shall, by reason of our social and economic structure, continue to deny the principles of one man, one value. How long shall we continue to live this life of contradictions? How long shall we

> continue to deny equality in our social and economic life. If we continue to deny it for long, we will do so only by putting our political democracy in peril. We must remove this contradiction at the earliest possible moment or else those who suffer from inequality will blow up the structure of political democracy which this assembly has so laboriously built up.

Louis Henkin, President of the US Institute of Human Rights, wrote about constitutions:

> Constitutions to be sure, are at best promises, and constitutional promises often remain unfulfilled. But what a constitution promises tells us, at least, what a society pretends or aspires to, where individual rights stand in its political system and scale of values and about how rights fare in fact.

Ambedkar was practical and realistic in his approach. "No matter how good or bad a constitution may be," he said once, "much depends on who is implementing it and how it is implemented". The Constitution was framed with a view to making India a strong, united nation with a strong centre. Suffering from the ravages of partition, the prime need was to consolidate and secure its freedom. India was not a nation in the sense this is generally understood. Divided vertically and horizontally into thousands of castes and many religious and linguistic groups, it was difficult to mould it into a nation.

S.K. Biswas, in his article examining Ambedkar's contribution to drafting of the Indian Constitution, writes of how Ambedkar come to be selected as, at first, a member of the drafting committee that was to draft the Indian Constitution and later as its chairman. He discusses Ambedkar's thoughts and expectations regarding the new constitution that India was to have. In the process, he gives the proceedings of the Constituent Assembly as a constitution-making body, particularly the resolutions and decisions made to facilitate the adoption of a new constitution for India (see Annexure 11).

Alladi Krishnaswamy Ayyar[8], a member of the Drafting Committee, concluded his speech by saying:

> I would be failing in my duty if I do not express my high appreciation of the skill and ability with which my friend, the Hon. Dr. Ambedkar, has piloted this constitution and his untiring work as the chairman of the Drafting Committee.

But there have also been views that Ambedkar's actual vision and ideas could never find a place in the framework of the new Constitution and he had to compromise in many respects.

Bhagwan Dass, advocate in the Supreme Court, stated:

> In spite of the fact that Dr. Ambedkar is called the principal architect of the Constitution, this was not the kind of Constitution he wanted to make for India. He had drafted a different kind of Constitution and circulated. Given a free hand he would have made a different kind of Constitution.

K.V. Rao was of the opinion that Ambedkar was not father but mother of the Indian Constitution. According to him, Ambedkar had no part in making decisions and far from germinating ideas, he had to compromise his own.

Works

Even while Ambedkar was involved seriously in his social struggle for the dalits, he authored several books. These not only spoke of the condition of the dalits in India and the efforts needed to free them of the caste oppression but also dealt with political and economic subjects. His main books were: *Castes in India*, 1916; *The Problem of the Rupee: Its Origin and its Solution*, March 1923; *Annihilation of Caste*, December 1935; *Thoughts on Pakistan*, December 1940; *What Congress and Gandhi Have Done to the Untouchables*, June 1945; *Who Were the Shudras?* October 1946; *The Untouchable*, October 1948; and *Buddha and his Dhamma*, published after his death in 1957.

The insults, inhuman treatment, indignities, discrimination and humiliation inflicted upon him by an unjust, ruthless and caste-ridden society—the Hindus, Muslims, Parsis and the Christians—gave him a shock such as he had never experienced before and it forced him to think about untouchability which before these incidents was with him a matter of course—as it was with many untouchables. These left an indelible impression on his mind.

There are innumerable heart-breaking events in the life of Ambedkar which he wrote in his diary, but he did not write a full autobiography.

When the biography *Dr. Ambedkar: Life and Mission* by Dhananjay Keer was published in May 1954 in the lifetime of Ambedkar, N.C. Rattu approached him with a complementary copy. At the time Ambedkar said. "What makes you so happy? Is there something special?" Rattu stammered: "Sir, here is your biography written by Dhananjay Keer." He held the book in his hand, took a quick glance at its contents and pored over a few pages. "The author", he said, "did meet me twice or thrice for clearing some points in relation to certain events, but this is not all that he has written. It is a long... very long... story." "Nobody", he said with a sigh, "can write" "anyhow," he said further, "he has made an attempt." "Then Sir," Rattu humbly said, "Why don't you write your autobiography when I am there to help and spare as much time as you may like." But due to the burden of work, Ambedkar could not complete his autobiography though he began the same.

Ambedkar's autobiography would have, no doubt, brought out an interesting account of his remininscences, had cruel death spared him for a couple of years.

In his reminiscences Ambedkar recalls, tearfully, the shocking experiences in his early life—such as at the Masur railway station on his way to Goregaon to meet his father with whom he was to spend his summer vacation and during his visits to Chalisgaon, Daulatabad Fort and other places. He also recalls, with a heavy heart, his sojourn in the Parsi inn and the service in the state of Baroda:

> I tell you I wept bitter tears on the day I was hounded out from place to place in Baroda, and even the memory of my days in Baroda fills my eyes with tears. Let me, however, tell you that I cannot be too grateful to his highness for what he has done for me.

On December, 6, 1956, Mrs. Ambedkar got up as usual, but she found her husband had passed away in sleep. His death was the result of severe diabetic neurosis.

Paying tributes Nehru said in the Lok Sabha that Ambedkar would be remembered mostly as a "symbol of revolt" against all the oppressing features of the Hindu society. *The Times*, London recognised his great efforts as a social reformer and said that his name would figure prominently in any history of the socio-political exploitation of India in the closing years of the British rule.

A.C. Rattu, one of the associates of Ambedkar, stated that almost all human beings run after the mirage of worldly pleasures and enjoyments that go on multiplying in some form or other, so much so that as one advances in age one becomes more attached to one's family, property and other material things. The manifold desires pierce him like the shaft of an arrow. It is said that a man himself may be sure to pass through the eye of the needle, but not while laden with his desires and ambitions. History will, however, be a witness and bear testimony to historians, research scholars and future generations of how Ambedkar, in his old age, unmindful of his only son, grandchildren, huge library and house and property, felt distressed, sobbed and wept, foreseeing the gloomy future in store for his downtrodden brethren. He was sad that the poor and illiterate masses in the villages remained unchanged economically and continued to be subjected to harassment at the hands of the upper castes.

Ambedkar wanted to serve his country to the best of his ability, but those in power were not prepared to utilise his services due to age-old prejudices. This distressed him very much. There are few parallels in world history to such a unique personality.

Why No Nobel Prize for Ambedkar?

Om Prakash discusses in depth Ambedkar's contribution to economics and why he was not honoured with the Nobel Prize. He recognises Ambedkar as an economist par excellence, one of two luminaries—the other being Hugh Dalton of the London School of Economics who, migrating to politics, came to serve as Chancellor of the Exchequer in Britain's Labour Government after the historic general 1945 elections. He says, Ambedkar succeeded simultaneously in making the discipline of finance both scientifically sound and operationally meaningful, while adding to it a lot of literary flavour to attract academic interest in an otherwise dull area of study.

Ambedkar was the author of a number of treatises and articles on political subjects and especially economics. He moved to politics via law, and was Labour Member in Viceroy's Executive Council for four years (1942–46) and Minister for Law for another four years (1947–51) in the Government of India after independence. During the brief interlude (1946–47), he returned to the academic world for a while, bringing out his own model constitution for the proposed United States of India. However, his desire to bring out Volume II of *The History of Indian Currency and Banking* as a supplement to *The Problem of the Rupee* (published after 1923) remained unfulfilled.

He had accomplished the near impossible task of writing three dissertations within three years (1920–23).One was on "Provincial Decentralisation of Imperial Finance in British India" for the M.Sc. degree and another was on "The Problem of the Rupee: Its Origin and its Solutions" (submitted in 1923 to London University for his D.Sc. degree.)

Within two years, another monumental work entitled *The Evaluation of Provincial Finance in British India: A Study of Provincial Decentralisation of Imperial Preference* was brought out by publishers King & Son in London in 1925. By that time, Ambedkar had risen to the top echelon as a qualified economist of Indian origin.

But law and politics took most of his time over the next three decades except for a breathing spell during 1946–47 when he got his D.Sc. thesis reprinted. Yet, he was able to contribute to economic thinking through a score of books including *Small Holdings in India and their Remedies*, *Federation vs Freedom*, *States and Minorities* and *Annihilation of Caste* (edited by Mulk Raj Anand in 1990), besides his intellectual perceptions incorporated into the Constitution as enforced in 1950.

While prefacing "The Problem of the Rupee", Ambedkar crossed swords with J.M. Keynes, Britain's prophet economist, saying:

> On the theoretical side, there is no other book except that of Professor Keynes which makes any attempt to examine its scientific basis. But the conclusions he has arrived at are in sharp conflict with those of mine. Our differences extend to almost every proposition that he has advanced in favour of the exchange standard. This difference proceeds from the fundamental fact which seems to be overlooked by Professor Keynes, that nothing will stabilise the rupee unless we stabilise its general purchasing power. That the exchange standard does not do. It concerns itself only with symptoms and does not go to the disease. Indeed, on my showing if anything it aggravates the disease.

Edwing Cannan, in his foreword, criticised Ambedkar, but accepted the latter's originality and practical wisdom in the following words:

> I do not share Mr. Ambedkar's hostility to the system, nor accept most of his arguments. But he hits some nails very squarely on the head and even when I have thought him quite wrong, I have found a stimulating freshness in his views and reasons. An old teacher like myself learns to tolerate the vagaries of originality, even when they resist severe examination such as that of which Mr. Ambedkar speaks. In practical conclusion, I am inclined to think he is right.

Taking the period 1875–76 to 1891–92 as a case in point, Ambedkar expressed concern at the depreciation in the external value of the rupee from 21.63 pence to 16.73 pence. About the same time, as he noted, India's sterling debt and rupee debt roughly grew three-fold and two-fold, respectively.

As such, Ambedkar's thesis propounded some seventy years ago is crucially valid today: first, that inflation at home is bound to erode the external value of the rupee; and, secondly, that such depreciation which bolsters the rupee burden of foreign debt is not in India's national interest.

Ambedkar's treatise on "Provincial Finance" started with an invigorating preface: "For a long time to come students will be saved the conventional humiliation of making an apology for presenting a study of Indian Finance or Economics." It was supported by a powerful foreword from the Columbia Professor, Edward R.A. Seligman, who testified: "The problem discussed by Mr. Ambedkar in his excellent dissertation is one that is arousing a growing interest in all parts of the world."

Tracing the evolution of provincial finance in India, Ambedkar identified three eras over a period of fifty years: (a) Budget by Assignments (1871–77), (b) Budget by Assigned Revenues (1877–82), and (c) Budget by Shared Revenues (1882–1921). The first period was associated with rigidity, since revenue assignment remained fixed whereas expenditure tended to grow, more so with the fall in the purchasing power of the rupee. The second phase provided some scope of flexibility with better management of revenue realisation under certain heads, on the part of provincial (state) governments. During the third stage a good many sources of revenue were wholly provincialised. Presenting a critique of the change, Ambedkar opined: "It is obvious that good administration depends upon good finance; for finance is the fuel of the whole administrative machine." In fact, his book formed the cornerstone of federal finance in India.

To him, finance was not mere arithmetic; it was a great policy leading ultimately, in 1950, to the constitutional provision of the quinquennial Finance Commissions and the emergence of the Gadgil Formula (sought to be revised again in 1990).

Ambedkar, in his own model constitution, had dreamt of a socialist structure based, *inter alia*, on: (a) nationalisation of all key industries, (b) nationalisation of all land, along with adoption of collective farming, particularly for the benefit of the landless rural population, and (c) state monopoly of insurance, with compulsory life insurance for every citizen of India. But such a ginger approach could not be pushed through the Constituent Assembly, even though Ambedkar came to be Chairman of the Drafting Committee.

In spite of his socialist manifesto, Ambedkar did not favour an ostentation of austerity. In 1937, he criticised the then Bombay government's move to lower the salaries of ministers to just Rs. 500 per month. As a member of the Legislative Assembly, he asserted that "nobody is going to be deceived by all these things." He put forward four arguments favouring higher salaries: (a) social standard, (b) competency, (c) democracy (with a sense of responsibility), and (d) integrity and purity of administration.

Ambedkar also implored the government to give up the greed for revenue from excise on liquor. He pressed for the implementation of the prohibition policy to save human beings from demoralisation and to upgrade the quality of life.

Ambedkar can be compared, on the one hand, with Karl Marx as a socio-political-economic crusader and, on the other, with Lord Keynes, as a monetary and financial economist. None of these thinkers could complete the biblical span of seventy years. The death of Marx coincided with the birth of Keynes, for whom Ambedkar was a younger contemporary.

The USSR witnessed the first major challenge to Marx in 1985, followed by the collapse of many other Marxian systems (with China still a major exception) by 1989–90. The dream of Keynes to have an international currency may well be on the verge of partial fulfilment. But his doctrine of deficit financing, having brought misery to many developing and even developed countries, had fallen from grace even before the Marxian debacle. The theory of trickle-down, having virtually failed to ameliorate the socio-economic lot of the masses in spite of massive capital investment, met with the same fate. However, Ambedkar's anti-inflation thesis is still valid and crucially relevant for the Indian economy.

In the days of Marx, there was no Nobel Prize at all. When Keynes and Ambedkar were writing, it did exist, but the discipline of economics was not covered by it. The Nobel Prize for Economics came to be instituted as late as 1969. More recently, financial economics has come to be recognised as a separate sub-discipline, with Modigliani of MIT leading in 1985, followed by Markowitz, Miller and Sharp—the three who shared the Nobel Prize of 1990. Ambedkar was, certainly, a formidable forerunner on this score.

It is not easy to compare the lives of King and Ambedkar, two great reformers of the twentieth century who launched a socio-political movement of great significance for the downtrodden people in their countries, as they were placed against different backgrounds and waged their struggle in differing contexts. King fought against the segregation and discrimination of blacks by the dominant whites of America (a struggle against racial injustice) and Ambedkar against the exploitation of the dalits by Hindus (a struggle against caste-based injustice). However, a close analysis of their political movements for social freedom, equality and justice for their downtrodden communities brings out interesting similarities. Both King and Ambedkar emerged as leaders due to circumstances, i.e., in response to a certain prevailing situation in society and at a crucial period in their country's historical growth. It was a time when even after some positive development over the years, the condition of the blacks in America and the dalits in India was miserable. Both the men had the courage to put their struggle before any kind of personal ambition. Logical men of great moral stature, they dedicated their lives to the service of their fellowmen. Refusing to believe that a human being could be inferior on the basis of his birth, they led the downtrodden people of their society into the streets to protest against various forms of discrimination and injustices. Both were visionaries who knew that only by co-operation and mutual goodwill, could the different races and castes harmoniously coexist in society.

A detailed study of their movements shows how and why their movements were able to unite the suffering blacks and dalits in their struggle for liberation from centuries of oppression and how they were able to succeed where others would have failed.

Once Baba Saheb Ambedkar wrote:

> Who can be called a great man? If asked of military heroes such as Alexander, Attila, Ceaser and Tamerlane, the question is not difficult to answer. The military men make epochs and effect vast transitions. They appeal and dazzle their contemporaries by their resounding victories. They become great without waiting to be called great. As the lion is among the deer, so they are among men. But it is equally true that their permanent effect on the history of mankind is very small. Their conquests shrink, and even so great a general as Napoleon after all his conquests left France smaller than he

found it. When viewed from a distance they are seen to be only periodical, if necessary, incidents in the world's movement, leaving no permanent mark on the character of the society in which they live. The details of their career and their morals may be interesting, but they do not affect society and form no leaven to transform or temper the whole.

Sincerity must be the test of a great man. Clemenceau once said that most statesmen are rogues. Statesmen are not necessarily great men, and obviously those on whose experience he founded his opinion must have been those wanting in sincerity. Nonetheless no one can accept that sincerity is the primary or the sole test, for sincerity is not enough. A great man must have sincerity. For it is the sum of all moral qualities without which no man can be called great. But there must be something more than mere sincerity in a man to make him great. A man may be sincere and yet he may be a fool, and a fool is the very antithesis of a great man. A man is great because he finds a way to save society in its hours of crises. But what can help him to find the way? He can do so only with the help of intellect. Intellect is the light. Nothing else can be of any avail. It is quite obvious that without the combination of sincerity and intellect no man can be great. Is this enough to constitute a great man? At this stage we must, I think, make a distinction between an eminent individual and a great man. For I am certain that a great man is something very different from an eminent individual. Sincerity and intellect are enough to mark out an individual as being eminent as compared to his fellows. But they are not enough to raise him to the dignity of a great man. A great man must have something more than what a merely eminent individual has. What must be that thing? Here comes the importance of the philosopher's definition of a great man. A great man must be motivated by the dynamics of a social purpose and must act as the scourge and the scavenger of society. These are the elements which distinguish an eminent individual from a great man and constitute his title-deeds to respect and reverence.

5

Conclusion

A study of the history of race relations in the West and particularly America and caste relations in India in a comparative perspective reveals a complex pattern of factors involved in the origin of race and caste conflict in these societies. Such generalisation in tracing factors responsible for two different kinds of conflicts in two diverse societies is possible as remarkably similar processes of general evolution and development are to be found between race relations in America—which in a way epitomises the white-black struggle in the West—and caste relations in India.

Contrary to what some historians and thinkers maintain, it is difficult to blandly suggest that there exists abstract and natural antipathy among different racial and caste groups which is responsible for tensions amongst them. The earliest Aryan society in the Indian subcontinent discriminated between groups on the basis of 'varna' which literally meant 'colour'. At this stage, there was a great deal of inter-mixture with the dasyus, for instance, though at the same time such inter-mixture was not encouraged. The *Rigveda* does not indicate development of a strict caste hierarchy in Aryan society. Caste rigidity became a feature of the Aryan society in later times when attempts to bypass the caste system were seen as sacrilegious especially as the inflexible system had been authenticated by Hindu sacred scriptures including the *Puranas*, the epic literature and the *Dharmashastras*. It was the expectation that the political and economic factors that emerged with the growth of civilisation, the rise of big cities and prosperous trade and commerce activities could lessen the caste system but the so-called modernity played a major role in strengthening of the caste system. It was in the interests of the brahmins to keep another group—the sudras—suppressed in society in order to ensure their social and economic superiority. So also, Europeans in the early middle ages formed no conclusions about their racial superiority. Even at the stage where they had gained control of new lands in the Americas after a bitter struggle with the natives to expand their economic activities, though they regarded the coloured people as inferior, they did not form fixed opinions about any inherent biological or cultural incapacity of these people. But later with increasing political domination and prospects for greater commerce and economic wealth, the nationalistic powers of Europe started justifying their political and economic designs upon the colonised with subtle theories of racial masterhood. It can well be questioned whether decline of the Roman Catholic Church with its mystical inhibitions to free exploitation of economic resources encouraged the theories rationalising in-born human inferiority or the decline of the Roman Catholic Church was a result of its harsh views proving a religious obstacle to nations' growing economic prosperity. The task of building up America, which required cheap and strong labour for exploiting its rich natural resources, gave a fillip to black slavery. Thus, both caste and race rivalry were fuelled and maintained over centuries. The last two centuries, however, signify a turning point.

Under the British, in the Indian subcontinent, the caste system became clear-cut, with each caste having its place in the caste hierarchy; and so, caste differences became sharper and more easily questionable. A few western-educated Indian scholars, for instance, begun to question the evils of the Indian caste system and advocate social reform to rid the society of untouchability and caste-based exploitation. Similarly, though racial antagonism attained maturity during the latter half of the nineteenth century, it was coupled with attempts by both black and white leaders in America to abolish black exploitation.

Throughout the decades of the twentieth century, there have been efforts worldwide to emphasise equality between all men and human rights for all. The crusade against race and caste discrimination intensified with great leaders and thinkers coming to the forefront to disapprove its practice in society. In America, the blacks' struggle for civil rights and equality with whites was led by men like Martin Luther King who believed in integration of the two communities in the democratic society of America so that they could live in amity without mutual feelings of hatred and fear. For this, it was necessary for blacks to not only ensure changes in the laws that had always affirmed white superiority but also convince others through their behaviour and values that they were in no way inferior to other communities. Whites, on the other hand, had to accept psychologically and otherwise blacks' right to equality and make the necessary changes in the rule books. But the trend of white liberalism especially in the post-1960s was, in a way, a setback to the equality issue as it stressed national redemption more than the actual issue of self-sufficiency and equality for blacks; in other words, racial reform was evaluated by its usefulness to the moral profile of the whites, than by its relevance for blacks' development. Thus their affirmative action resulted in group preferences and entitlements for the blacks like admission preferences in universities without a policy focusing on the blacks' educational development before college. Such preferences did not deliver as the blacks were not held to the same standards as whites. The same kind of problem can be seen in the Indian caste scenario. The ideas and activities of the national leaders of independence and social reformers appealed to the popular imagination in an attempt to undo the evils of the caste system. They succeeded to a great extent in breaking down the narrow outlook of the upper caste strata. In the pre-independence decades, there was an upsurge among dalits to fight against centuries of oppression and win equality and respect for themselves in society. This was possible as they were led by able leaders like Jyotiba Phooley and B.R. Ambedkar who were willing to sacrifice their all for the task. The policy of reservations for downtrodden groups was actually meant to serve in this context. Here too, though these castes have continued to have a presence in universities offering prestigious courses and employment preferences at different levels and in different areas, they are not held to the same standards as the Hindu. Whether it be the blacks in America or the dalits in India, the general feeling is that they do not deserve to be where they are but have gained their place in society due to the preferences and entitlements. Realising that actual equality would be compromised and full interaction would not be possible if equal rights and respect and self-sufficiency for these communities is not kept as the one and only goal, both King and Ambedkar did not favour the policy of preferments. In the case of Ambedkar, though he was the major force behind the introduction of reservation policy in the constitutional agenda, he knew that the implementation of the policy would provide some relief to the downtrodden but it was not a lasting solution. That is why most of the persons having higher posts were not interested to provide the facilities to the dalits. And Ambedkar personally opted for religious conversion and encouraged his followers to do the same, his view being that equality of right and status with the upper castes was not possible for the untouchables within the Hindu religion with its inherent caste structure.

The present-day situation with regard to problems of race and caste discrimination needs some careful scrutiny. The last century saw modernisation on a vast scale—relating to political systems, of living standards, of health, art, rather culture as a whole. Technological advancements especially in communication and cultural economic liberation has made the world literally a global village. Integration, respect for human freedom and dignity and peace have been the key words with incessant calls for preserving human rights, safeguarding the earth's environment, sustainable development and saving the world from violence especially in the form of terrorism and nuclear catastrophes. The wave of progression and enlightenment has brought about a general change in the approach and attitude of the people towards the reigning concerns. In the western as well as the eastern world, societies with some specific exceptions are now more tolerant of each other's values; the people are themselves adopting to global changes and embracing democratic values.

Now, racial and caste prejudices are being washed away as is evident from inter-mixing, inter-dining and even inter-marriage among different racial and caste communities. In urban Indian society, for instance, people are not particular about caste affiliations; what has taken the place of prominence is social and economic status of group.

However, the issue of discrimination persists and all is not as simple as it seems. Today, the situation of racial conflict in American society is much more serious as well as caste antipathy in India.

Inter-mixing of races in American society is still selective; for one, the disparities in social and economic status are too marked to allow it. And then there are what we call the psychological factors. The blacks and the whites continue to be identified as two separate groups with little in common and this simple identification helps in contributing to the racial problem. In Indian society, in contrast, the caste system is a complex phenomenon: the upper castes imply a number of castes in different regions of India, all diverse from one another in food habits, customs, way of life though there are general similarities. In the last fifty years, many dalits have gained political ascendancy and due to benefits like the reservation policy, enjoy a good socio-economic status particularly in some states. In urban centres, the caste differences get blurred in day-to-day life though in rural areas of states like Bihar, Andhra Pradesh and Uttar Pradesh, the caste rivalry is very much real.

The 'burden of the past' is a factor responsible for continued racial and caste tensions; this factor is specially relevant in the American context as, according to some thinkers, it has become a part of the white American psyche and is reflected in the white American's response and attitude towards the black American.

The caste-Hindus of India and the whites in America who have always claimed superiority feel a moral obligation to make up for their past 'actions' and so they are quite ready to compromise by giving the long-suppressed groups some kind of leverage. Though this appeases their conscience, it does not mean that they believe the oppressed groups deserve the benefits.

The past lies still more heavily on the white American shoulder. This is because of the identification of blacks with Africa as the land of their origin. The truth is that the Negroes were imported into America to do hard menial job in white plantations and industries. While the blacks slaved getting the barest minimum in return, their white masters grew wealthier by the day. This truth gets lost when the white American feels that the blacks bear racial and cultural affinity with the Africans and so are less truly American than the whites. Where the white extremist groups are concerned, this totally purges their conscience of past sins and establishes the status of the blacks as second-class citizens.

According to one view, the Americans have reformed their society. They have given the opportunity to the blacks in different fields especially in literature, sport and industry. industrialists in America allowed participation to blacks in their establishments. In India some industrialists like Bharat Ram have given statements that if the central government compelled them, they would give reservation, in private sector to dalits. They would give only salary, not participation. It means that they do not want the involvement of dalits in private sector.

ANNEXURES

ANNEXURES 1
(Quoted from Lamar Alexander, *Policy Review*, November–December 1998)

American century comes to a close, we are losing our ability to say what it means to be an American. We are forgetting the handful of compelling ideas that have forged individuals from so many backgrounds into one nation, indivisible....... We are Italian, American, Chinese-American, African-American, Scots- Irish-American. There are so many hyphenated versions of us we can hardly keep count. We cherish our regional accents, research our family roots, and burst with pride at ethnic dinners. We are proud of where we have arrived from, and rightly so, but we are forgetting that we have always been producer of where we have arrived; producer of saying, "We are all Americans."

The latest symptom of the divisive tendency is President Clinton's Commission on Race. It issued its final report, the culmination of 14 months of 'dialogue' involving 17,000 Americans in 39 states, which signed that America suffers from too little race-consciousness. And its recommended remedy? More race-consciousness.

Before issuing his report, Commission Chairman John Hope Franklin wrote to the President: "The idea that we should aspire to a color-blind society is an impediment to reducing racial stereotyping.... The best way to reduce racial stereotyping is to be conscious of racial differences." The report recommends that the President make this all-race-all-the-time approach to national unity permanent by institutionalising his Commission on Race. The proposed 'President's Council for One America' would pick up where the commission left off: carrying on the "great and unprecedented conversation about race."

This is the wrong conversation. As I understand where the President is coming from, considering where he grew up, and where John Hope Franklin grew up, and where I grew up. No southerner who has experienced the indignity of black Americans being pushed to the back of the bus, sent to separate hospitals, relegated to separate bathrooms, and kept out of many of the best schools and colleges because of their race can remain indifferent to the legacy of discrimination. And no one can look at our elite college campuses today, at the board rooms of Fortune 500 companies, and at those who seem permanently consigned to lower paying jobs, without wanting to open opportunity to Americans of all races.

But the President has started the wrong conversation. With all due respect, he has the wrong ideas about what it means to be an American. In his 1997 State of the Union address, the President said America's greatest strength is its diversity. He must have been the first President of the United States ever to say that, and I hope he will be the last.

Of course, diversity can be a great strength. But diversity is not America's greatest strength. Bosnia is diverse. Rwanda is diverse. Quebec is diverse. Racial and ethnic differences are tearing those places apart. America's greatest strength is that we are the only nation that, as Margaret Thatcher observed, "has so successfully combined people of so many different races and nations within a single culture."

So shouldn't our national conversation be about what pulls us apart? Think about the times when America has been at her best: winning our freedom at Lexington and Concord, defending that freedom on the beaches of Normandy, and marching together in Selma, Alabama, to secure freedoms for every American. During those times we united around a common set of principles: equal opportunity, individual rights, self-government. From these principles flows the path to racial reconciliation.

ANNEXURE 2
(Quoted from Shelby Steele, How Liberals Debase Black Achievement, *Policy Review*, November-December 1998)

Racial Virtuousness

A fundamental weakness of post-1960s liberalism has been its greater preoccupation with national redemption than with what it actually takes for blacks to achieve self-sufficiency and equality. The great ingenuity of interventions like affirmative action has not been that they give Americans a way to identify with the struggle of blacks, but that they give them a way to identify with racial virtuousness quite apart from blacks.

It is a mistake to think that only blacks know segregation. Whites know it, too, not as its victims but as its open perpetrators. But it made whites know—on some level—how simple a thing evil is, how ordinary, how close at hand, how compellingly convenient it can be. This kind of knowledge makes for its own urgency—an urgency coming out of the experience of segregation and racism. And in the United States this is the urgency that parallels, but then diverges from, the urgency that blacks feel for full equality. Two experiences of American racism, and two kinds of redemption needed—one from the shame of living with or practicing racism, the other from the shame of being subjugated by it.

I believe it is the former urgency that drives the liberalism of many people. A great confusion in American liberalism after the 1960s comes from the fact that the white mandate for redemption can only fulfill itself through a concern for black equality. This has given us a liberalism that treats black equality more as a means to white moral authority than as an end in its own right. So we often end up evaluating racial reform more by its usefulness to the moral profile of whites than by how well it develops blacks. Universities across the country offer admission preferences to black students, yet this student group has the highest dropout rate and lowest grade-point average of any student group. If black equality were truly the goal, wouldn't policy focus on educational development before college? And if equality of performance between blacks and whites were the goal, wouldn't blacks be held to the same standards as whites precisely so they could achieve that equality?

The Helpless Black

This same white need for moral authority has also given government and other institutions an obsession with an equality of results. An equality of colours and numbers, a language of "diversity" and "multiculturalism," lets institutions engineer the beautiful picture of equality while pushing aside the black need to develop it.

But then, once in the colour-and-numbers game, the full and complex humanity of blacks—who they really are and what they really need—becomes inconvenient. And this is where the pursuit of moral authority ends in something both pernicious and paradoxical. In the world of interventionism, with all its schemes, formulas, and structural manipulations, blacks are relegated to that most alienated of human categories, "the other." Here they are seen as a different kind of humanity, as essentially unlike "mainstream" white humanity. And the essence of this "otherness" is their injuredness and helpessness. Because the interventions are justified by, and respond to, only these qualities, helplessness becomes the identity they are recognised for. It is the identity that makes them useful in the larger drama of white institutional redemption. In a sense otherness and inferiority now bring entry where they once caused exclusion. But in both cases—white racism or white redemption—blacks remain largely invisible beyond a presumed inferiority.

In post-1960s liberalism it is virtuous to be tolerant of black weakness and to think of blacks as "helpless others" as a way of acknowledging the historic evil of white racism. In other words, this liberalism tolerates black weakness and inferiority because they are the result of white evil. The liberal who has high expectations for his or her own children often feels that he or she cannot "push the issue" with blacks. The white mandate for redemption pressures the liberal to tolerate what holds blacks down. And, in this circuitous way, this liberalism endorses a kind of racism. Double standards, preferential treatment, provisions for "cultural difference" and various kinds of entitlement all constitute a pattern of exceptionalism that keeps blacks (and other minorities) down by tolerating weakness at every juncture where strength is expected of others...

The Costs of White Intervention

The idea of a black openly outside the framework of liberalism is still odd in the United States. Such a person seems to be disqualifying himself from the fruits of America's struggle for racial redemption, standing against his own racial self-interest... I believe that preferential treatment is essentially a white liberal idea of black self-interest that serves institutions by letting them practice exceptionalism, while blacks have their weakness tolerated rather than strength rewarded. Then, after black weakness has been massaged, accepted, understood, and felt for, people wonder why the infamous gap between blacks and whites on tests and other performance measures won't close. The answer, of course, is that nobody seriously asks that it be closed. A defining paradox of post-1960s liberalism is the symbiotic bond between the moral authority of America's institutions and black inferiority...

From the abolitionist era to the present, the terms of racial reform in America have always been set by a coalition of white liberals and black leaders. And since the 1960s, interventionism that would engineer blacks to equality has been the virtuous idea of this coalition. But, in supporting interventionism, I think the black leadership has forsaken the black mandate to achieve true and full equality with all others for the perquisites of interventionism—the preferential patronage of jobs, careers, grant money, set-asides, diversity consulting businesses, black political districts, and so on. The black leadership, which could have emphasised anti-discrimination and black development as the road to black advancement, chose instead to rely primarily on group preferences and entitlement. This bargain has transformed the civil rights establishment into something of a grievance elite, largely concerned with turning the exceptionalism practiced by institutions in regard to blacks into the patronage of racial preferences.

It is true that interventionism is what white society offered blacks (rather than serious anti-discrimination and development) because the redeeming look of equality could more easily be engineered this way. And the black leadership, coming out of segregation, in which whites had never given much of anything to the black cause, quickly grabbed up interventionism as a valid way to equality. Thus, for entirely opportune reasons, this post-1960s coalition of white liberals and black leaders made equality into a near perfect expediency with no relationship to a human equivalency between the races. As such it could be manufactured without the actual development of blacks to equality... This, of course, is the white liberal's crucible—he gets to define America's racial reform as interventionism, but he lives without even enough moral authority to declare himself racially innocent and have the declaration stand...

Black Conservatism, White Redemption

One of the great attractions of "conservatism" for blacks today is the freedom it offers from yet another white mandate—not white supremacy but white redemption.

History imposes these mandates on whites and blacks in the form of responsibilities that individuals in each group carry as a part of their racial identity. They are, I believe, absolute. They are more often denied than not by both whites and blacks, but even the denial validates their presence. Today the mere knowledge of what whites did to blacks in history makes whites responsible for showing a moral superiority to their race's behavior in the past. Correspondingly, the mere knowledge of an historically imposed inferiority makes blacks today responsible for showing an equality of achievement that their forebears were prevented from showing. History defines our identities as much by the collective responsibilities it imposes as by the selected tales of glory we take pride in. And these two mandated responsibilities—white redemption and black equality may be unwelcome and will often seem irrational, yet they are at the heart of what it means to be white and black in the United States.

But all this is a problem for the white liberal because he distinguishes himself from other whites by the intensity of his responsibility to the mandate. This intensity is his identity as a white liberal. He is not just accepting of this responsibility, he is passionate about it. Passionate moral responsibility is his trademark. Probably this is because passion seems the only correct response to great historical injustice, the least one can offer in payment for redemption. But the problem with an identity based on passion is that it often puts one at odds with reason and common sense.

However, an important qualification must be made here. Though the liberal identity calls for passion, real social passion is all but impossible to sustain over time. And so, like religious fervor, it must be codified into manners and practices so that the liberal can "genuflect." These genuflections, then, are the ritualised display of passionate responsibility to the white mandate of redemption. And this, as it were, is not a bad definition of "political correctness." The great problem this poses for liberalism, as for religion, is that when the original passion is reduced to genuflection, it is achieved more by mere conformity than by difficult effort. This introduces the same hollowness into liberalism that is the bane of organised religion—passion as conformity, iconography, and empty observance.

This has made post-1960s liberalism essentially a received doctrine, more autocratic than democratic. Amorphous and empty ideas like multiculturalism and diversity do not exist to be defined or debated so much as affirmed as received expressions of virtue...

The ritualisation of liberal passion has hardened it into a brittle mask. CEOs, foundation presidents, government officials, educators, politicians, union leaders, and the man and woman in the street—all can wear the mask of a racial progressive. In a received liberalism of genuflection, true reform itself is simply not necessary.

One of the serious problems that this overall rigidity has brought to post-1960s liberalism is a confusion between its broad mandate and the means it uses to achieve it—that is, the assumption that a given intervention is the same thing as the white mandate for redemption. And from this confusion comes the liberal tendency to fight for interventions as though fighting for redemption itself, never realising that there might be many routes to the fulfillment of this mandate.

The "Glazer Trap"

I will call this confusion the "Glazer trap" in honor of the social critic Nathan Glazer, a man whose work I have often admired. Back in the mid-1970s, in a famous book called *Affirmative Discrimination,* Nathan Glazer launched one of the first thoughtful attacks on affirmative action. He was ahead of his time in arguing openly that affirmative action had moved dangerously from "equal opportunity to statistical parity." Like other neoconservatives, Glazer was a liberal who had become disenchanted with affirmative action as an intervention. He was not against the white mandate per se, the idea that restored moral authority in the United States would require serious racial reform. His objection, quite reasonably, was to the intervention of affirmative action as a means to that mandate.

The "Glazer trap," this confusion of intervention with mandate, comes from the calcification of liberal passion into mere propriety and iconography. And in the hardened and reflexive manners of contemporary liberalism, affirmative action is not simply one idea of reform among many; it is an icon of white American racial redemption. Moreover, as an icon, people are called upon to genuflect on it, not to examine it. We don't analyse it as we do economic policy because its only real accountability is to white American redemption, not economic prosperity. And that redemption is won through conformity and genuflection, not the effectiveness of the policy. (President Clinton gets credit for supporting affirmative action, not for making it work.)

Conservative Confusion

But the "Glazer trap" goes well beyond liberals. Conservatives, too, have let the intervention of affirmative action be confused with the white mandate for redemption... If they attacked the intervention, it would seem as though they were rejecting the larger mandate that called for white America to seek redemption through racial reform. Thus, they had no way of attacking affirmative action without seeming racist.

The "Glazer trap" is in many ways the larger white American trap. White America has simply lacked the moral authority to confront the liberal fusion of intervention and mandate of affirmative action and white redemption. Republicans have been no more able than Democrats to say openly that affirmative action is only an intervention, a method, and not representative of America's larger will to redeem itself racially.

The reason America needs racial redemption in the first place is also the reason for our brittle post-1960s liberalism and the "trap" it produces. America's racial history has injured the very legitimacy of institutional America where race is concerned. Unable even to change the method of reform without seeming to forsake the redemptive mandate means that the United States can not carry out racial reform with integrity. Two things have not been possible: reform that works inside the framework of democratic principles, and reform that makes the difficult demands on former victims that are actually necessary for them to achieve parity. Post-1960s liberalism has been undermined, and to a large degree corrupted, by having to live within these impossible parameters. Unable to enforce either principles or difficulty, it has had to let the black grievance elite call the tune. And this elite has been quite happy not only to entrench preferential treatment for blacks as the predominant mode of reform but also to use preferences as a kind of patronage to insure its own power.

The lack of moral authority that racial reform hopes to overcome also makes integrity (and therefore effectiveness) impossible in such reform. This leads to the other side of the "trap" in which the liberal's good intentions undermine the good, in which he or she makes a virtue of discarding principles and suspending difficulty. On this side of the trap the liberal pursues racial redemption embarking on a kind of corruption. Listen to the leaders of America's institutions speak on race—the president of U.C. Berkeley saying he wants to create "multicultural atmospheres"—and you hear beneath the good multicultural intention the corruption of human engineering, of a university picking and choosing among human beings by skin colour alone, a racially sensitive atmosphere created by human insensitivity, corruption in the service of "good." Without the moral authority to reform by principle, we end up with an insecure, defensive, and often corrupt liberalism, not of reform but of apology.

ANNEXURE 3
(Quoted from Oliver C. Cox, *Caste, Class and Race*, Modern Reader Paperbacks, New York, 1948)

It is generally recognised that Sir Herbert Risley has been the most insistent advocate of the racial theory of caste. He did considerable anthropometrical research among the Hindus, using his racial hypothesis as a guide. However, the reliability of his data and the validity of his conclusions have been questioned by later observers.[1] There remains, then, only his hypothesis supported by deductive reasoning. Risley puts his theory in the form of a law of race contact.[2] It runs roughly as follows: White men in contact with people of color will take women from the colored group but will not give their own women. When the whites have bred enough white women, "they will close their ranks" and form a superior caste. The mixed bloods will then close their ranks, forming additional castes with degrees of superiority based upon lightness of color... In fact, what Risley has really achieved is an explanation of caste in terms of race relations and, having done so, he called race relations caste. Nripendra Kumar Dutt, writing more recently on the origin of caste, presents a variation of Risley, but his approach is somewhat historical. Let us consider this:

That the color question was at the root of the varna system is apparent from the meaning of the world *varna* (complexion) and from the great emphasis with which the Vedic Indians distinguished themselves from the non-Aryans in respect to color. The class which retained the utmost purity of color by avoiding intermixture naturally gained precedence in the social scale. The Brahmans were white, the Kashtriyas red, the Vaisyas—because of large absorption of black blood—were yellowish like the mulattoes of America, and the Sudras black, as is described in the Mahabharata.

> In the first stage the Indo-Aryans were divided into three orders or varnas. They had no scruple in marrying indiscriminately among themselves, while racial hatred made

them avoid contact with the non-Aryan Sudras. The memory of this age is preserved in the Mahabharata, Anushasana Parva, where it is stated that "The son of a Brahman by wives of the three varnas is a Brahman. Only four varnas are known to exist; a fifth does not exist." In other words the son invariably belonged to the order of his father, whatever might be the rank of his mother. Such a statement is not subscribed to by any of the Dharmasastras. As, however, the Vaisyas came into greater association with the Sudras and became more polluted with non-Aryan blood than the two other classes, aversion came to be felt towards the union in marriage with a Vaisya girl.

This state of caste development is represented in a *sloka* of the same Anushasana Parva which states that: "Of the four wives of four orders of a Brahman, in the two higher he himself (i.e. a Brahman) is born, in the two lower less pure sons are born who belong to their mother's varna." This state of things evidently continued till about the time of Manu, who also does not assign a separate caste to the son of a Brahman father and a Kshatriya mother. With the hardening of caste rules in the course of time, even this freedom was restricted. In the later Dharmasastras we find that none could become a Brahman who was not born of Brahman parentage on both sides. When the marriage with a Sudra woman was so much abhorred and blamed, we can easily conceive of the horror and detetestation which a Brahman in his *racial pride* would feel at the sight of a Brahman woman marrying a Sudra. No words are too strong to condemn such a marriage, and as a deterrent it is enacted that the issue of such a union should occupy the humblest position in society. Thus we see that the development of inter-caste marriage restrictions was principally due to the racial difference between white conquerors and the black, and the desire of the former to preserve their purity of blood.[3]

Dutt's hypothesis contains just about the whole gamut of spurious reasoning on this problem; therefore, it is particularly appropriate as a model for discussion...

Probably the most common explanation of the origin of caste is based upon beliefs that the word "varna" means color; hence, caste must have originated in the Aryan's passion for protecting their light Asiatic color from intermixture with the dark color of the Dravidians. However, as we shall attempt to indicate below, the early literature of the Hindus does not show this to be the case.

It becomes necessary for Dutt to rely upon even such remote metaphorical descriptions of the castes as white, red, yellow, and black. There is understandably some silence about explaining why the blood of the princes had already become "red" and only that of the priests had remained white—and this in spite of the fact that the Brahmans and the Kshatriyas intermarried freely. In fact, Professor Hopkins has shown that in the Vedic period the Kshatriyas were the ruling caste in India.[4] If we take these disconnected references to color as implying superiority, then "red" must have been superior to white. As we shall see below, the term "varna" has other meanings besides color.[5] The analogy with the mulattoes in America is rather astonishing but characteristic of these theories.

One assumption which seems fatal to these theories is that there were two colour castes before there were castes within any one colour group. Not only is this position unrevealed in the data, but also reliance upon it has led to such confused statements as: "The class which retained the utmost purity of colour by avoiding intermixture naturally gained precedence in the social scale." Why "naturally"? What does our writer mean by "class"? If it means caste, then castes were formed before they began to avoid colour mixture.

Let it be said that we have no record of the racial composition of Sudras. The term "Sudra" is not synonymous with "Dravidian". Neither do we have any authority for the statement: "Indo-Aryans had no scruple in marrying indiscriminately among themselves." The period is not known when a Vaisya man could freely marry a Brahman woman or even a Kshatriya woman. Only in the legendary narratives do kings wed the daughters of priests, but it is a platitude of the Mahabharata that no woman could marry into the caste beneath hers. Hopkins quotes the epic story of a Brahman woman and a king. Says the king: "Thou canst have no connubial connection with me, for thou shouldst not make a caste mixture."

Then, too, in spite of the assumed "horror" of mixture with the darker race, Brahman men were privileged to have wives from all three castes below them, Kshatriya from the two lower ones, and Vaisyas from the Sudras. Therefore, Brahmans may be said to have been the most flagrant mixers of blood in India. If colour were indeed the determining factor, is it possible to say that if a person happened to be white he ipso facto became a Brahman, if black, a Sudra, so that one might look upon a man and classify him unquestionably? The historical data do not sustain this possibility.

Notes

1. "Risley's conclusions, based on measurements made by him in Bengal, have been called in question by Crooke in the United Provinces, Enthoven in Bombay and Thurston in Madras, while O'Donnell has argued that even in Bengal measurements are often at variance with it." *Census of India*, 1911, Vol. I, Pt. I, p. 381. For further criticism, see *Census of India*, 1931, Vol. I, Pt. I, pp. 439 ff., and Vol. V, Pt. I, pp. 432 ff.
2. "Wherever in the history of the world one people has subdued another, whether by sudden invasion or by gradual occupation of their territory, the conquerors have taken the women of the country as concubines or wives, but have given their own daughters in marriage only among themselves. Where these two peoples are of the same race, or at any rate of the same color, this

initial stage of hypergamy soon passes away and complete amalgamation takes place. Where, on the other hand, marked distinctions of race and color intervene, and especially if the dominant people are continually recruited by men of their own blood, the course of evolution runs on different lines. The tendency then is toward the formation of a class of half-breeds, the result of irregular union between men of the higher and women of the lower, who marry only among themselves and are to all intents and purposes a caste. In this literal or physiological sense, caste is not confined to India. It occurs in a pronounced form in the Southern States of the American Republic, where Negroes, and the various mixed races, mulattoes, quadroons, and octoroons, each have a sharply restricted jus connubi of their own and are practically cut off from legal unions with the white race. The same set of phenomena may be observed among the half-breeds of Canada, Mexico, and South America, and among the Eurasians of India, who do not intermarry with the natives and only occasionally with pure-blood Europeans." *Imperial Gazetteer of India,* Vol.I, new ed., p. 345. See also *The People of India,* 2nd ed., pp. 5. G.S. Ghurye has criticised Risley's explanation but has himself presented a similar racial theory; see *Caste and Race in India,* p. 108.

3. *Origin and Growth of Caste in India,* Vol. I, pp. 21–23.
4. Edward W. Hopkins, "The Social and Military Position of the Ruling Caste in Ancient India", *Journal of American Oriental Society,* Vol. XIII, 1888.
5. It should be remarked that the criterion of a single word, 'varna' could never be accepted as adequate evidence of racial antagonism among Vedic Indians. Racial antagonism is a peculiar and complicated form of intergroup relationship, and it is this relationship which must be identified. We might just as well conclude that the Indo-Aryans ran locomotives in northwestern India because, let us say, the word 'steam' is frequently used in the Vedas.

ANNEXURE 4
(Quoted from Dhiru Bhai Sheth's draft paper for presentation at the conference on "Contemporary India in Transition" held at Lisbon, Portugal on 18–20 June, 1998)

The Portuguese 'discovery' of caste, however, went much beyond giving a name to India's varna jati system. The Portuguese were the first among Europeans to provide detailed accounts of its functioning. The most perceptive, empirical account of caste was given by the sixteenth century Portuguese, Duarte Barbosa. Barbosa identified the following main features of caste: (a) caste as a hierarchy, with Brahmans at the top and 'untouchables' at the bottom; (b) untouchability as linked to the idea of pollution; (c) existence of plurality of castes separated from each other by endogamy, occupation and commensality; (d) application of sanctions by castes to maintain their own customs and rules; (e) relationship of caste with political organisation.

Although Barbosa did not provide a systematic account, the elements of caste he identified remain central to any definition of caste. Moreover Barbosa's approach to reporting about caste had some distinctive qualities. First, he described caste as he saw it functioning on the ground; he got his facts by talking not just to the elites, but to common people in their own language. Second, he did not use the religious scriptures as a source of information on caste; there is no reference to the varna theory of caste in his narratives. Third, he related the idea of pollution to the practice of untouchability and not to functioning of the whole system. Fourth, he saw caste not exclusively in ritual-status terms, but also as a plurality of 'self-governing' cultural communities. Fifth, he stuck to a matter-of-fact account of what he saw and was told about caste, and refrained from moralising and passing value judgements on it.[1]

The Colonial Discourse

Nothing much of significance was added or any improvement made to Barbosa's account for the next 250 years by his European successors reporting on caste. It was only after the British rule was established in India that a second 'discovery' of caste was made by the Europeans. The Western Orientalist scholars, the Christian Missionaries and the British administrators began, in their different ways, to make sense of this complex phenomenon. A new, colonial discourse on caste was born. It marked important departures from pre-colonial accounts of caste. First, the new discourse centered on whether caste was a system beneficial to Indians or it worked against them. The Orientalist scholars viewed caste as serving some positive functions, whereas the Missionaries saw it as an unmitigated evil. Second, both its sympathisers and opponents, saw caste in highly schematised and unidimensional terms: as an inflexible hierarchy of vertically ranked ritual statuses. The idea of pollution which Barbosa saw in the context of untouchability was now generalised for the whole system in which the idea of ritual purity and impurity of statuses was considered the central principle governing the caste-system. The reality of caste was reconstructed largely from its depiction in the religious scriptures. In the event, Barbosa's empirical view of caste was now superimposed by the scriptural (ideological) varna view of caste. Third, with the 'discovery' of Hindu scriptures by the Orientalist scholars, caste became a prism through which the colonial rulers began to scc Indians and the whole Indian society: caste was now seen as representing a world view of Indians and a totality of India's social and cultural life. Certain non-ritual, even non-religious elements which always existed in the caste system and informed quite a few aspects of inter-caste relations, were theoretically ruled out of the system.

Fourth, in the course of setting-up its revenue administration, a number of land and village surveys were launched by the colonial regime in different regions of India. This focused the attention of revenue administrators, many of whom were anthropologically inclined scholars, on the Indian village—which was also a revenue unit. This focus developed into a view of village as the microcosm of the Indian society, and caste as constituting its social, economic and political organisation legitimated by its religious ideology.

In this village view of caste, caste was seen as an ensemble of local hierarchies, each contained within a village or a group of villages. This view contributed to the image of the village as a stable, unchanging social system. In the latter ethnographic studies of caste carried out by Indian sociologists, the *varna* theory was discarded, but caste continued to be seen as a vertical hierarchy of ritual statuses embedded in the religious and cultural context of the village.

Fifth, the administrative and anthropological concerns of the British officers led them to counter both the Orientalist and the Missionary views of caste. Their concern was utilitarian, about finding administrative and political ways to tame and change this formidable system functioning from ancient times, to suit needs of the colonial polity and economy. This concern of the colonialists prompted an ideological debate on caste. The debate achieved a degree of political sophistication which was not shown earlier either by the Orientalists in their appreciation or the Missionaries in their condemnation of the caste system. The debate introduced a new, theoretical- comparative dimension for viewing caste. Caste now began to be seen in comparison with normative (values of equality, individualism etc.) and social (estate, race, class etc.) categories of the Western societies. Eventually, with the English educated nationalist Indians joining the debate, on the terms set up by the colonial regime, caste became a bone of contention between conservatives and progressives, traditionalists and reformers. Valuation became the mode of observation.

Sixth, the method British administrators adopted in reporting about caste, unlike that of the Orientalist scholars, was 'empirical'. They did not see the caste system only in terms of the *varna* categories. They also saw castes as separate communities often divided by descent, political organisation and customs. Consequently, they theorised caste in terms of its racial and tribal origins and character. In fact, multiple and elaborate systems of classification of castes were evolved by them based on a variety of ethnographic materials, officially obtained through various village and caste surveys.[2] Seventh, crucial to the colonial discourse was the relationship between caste and the state. From the 1901 Census, the colonial state began caste-wise enumeration of the entire Indian population. The decennial censuses not only updated, every ten years, the population figures for every enumerated caste, but also gave it a specific name/label and a rank. In doing so, the census officers tended to rely on their 'reading' of the scriptures as well as local knowledge and practice. But when a name and/or a rank given to a caste was in dispute—and this happened frequently—the census officer's 'anthropological' judgement, albeit tempered by representations received from leaders of concerned caste, prevailed. Thus, despite the diversity of the debate, at the end of the day, the criterion of 'social precedence of one caste over the other' i.e. the scriptural principle of ritual status hierarchy, was explicitly and officially recognised.

The colonial state, thus, acquired an agency, even a legitimate authority, to arbitrate and fix the status claims made or contested by various castes about their locations in the ritual hierarchy. At the same time, the enumeration of castes and their ethnographic descriptions compiled by the State, highlighted how the social and economic advantages accrued to some castes and not to others in the traditional hierarchy. This led to demands among many castes for special recognition by the State for receiving educational and occupational benefits as well as for political representation. The colonial state assumed a dual role: of a super Brahmin who located and relocated disputed statuses of castes in the traditional hierarchy and of the just and modern ruler who wished to 'recognise' rights and aspirations of his weak and poor subjects. This helped the State to protect its colonial political economy from incursions of the emerging nationalist movement. Among other things, it also induced people to organise and represent their interests in politics in terms of caste identities and participate in the economy on the terms and through mechanisms set by the colonial regime.

On the whole, the colonial regime not only introduced new terms of discourse on caste, but also brought about some changes in the caste system itself. A large part of these changes, however, were unintended consequences of the colonial policies; they were related to the large historical forces of modernisation, secularisation and urbanisation which had begun to make some impact on the Indian society by the end of the nineteenth and the beginning of the twentieth century. But some specific policies of the colonial regime, aimed at delegitimising the power of the traditional social elites and creating support for its own rule, had direct consequences for the caste system. Towards the end of the colonial rule such policies alongside the larger historical forces had produced some profound and far-reaching changes in the caste system.[3]

The most important among the changes was the formation of a new, translocal identity among 'lower castes', collectively as a people with the consciousness of being 'oppressed' by the traditional system of hierarchy. The discourse of rights, until then quite alien to the concept governing ritual hierarchy, made its first appearance in the context of the caste system. New ideological categories like 'social justice' began to interrogate the idea of ritual purity and impurity according to which the traditional stratified system endowed entitlement and disprivileges to hereditary statuses. The established categories of ritual hierarchy began to be confronted with new categories like depressed and oppressed castes.[4] Second, several castes occupying more or less similar locations in different local hierarchies began to organise themselves horizontally into regional and national level associations and federations, as it became increasingly necessary for them to negotiate with the State and in the process project their larger social identity and numerical strength.[5]

Third, movements of the lower caste for upward social mobility, which were not new in the history of the caste system, acquired a qualitatively new dimension as they began to attack the very ideological foundations of the ritual hierarchy of castes, in terms not internal to the system (as the case with the Buddhist and Bhakti movements), but in the modern ideological terms of justice and equality.

Changes that occurred in the caste system during the colonial period have greatly intensified after India's de-colonisation. Further, with India establishing a liberal democratic State and the growth of institutions of competitive, representational democracy, the changes acquired newer dimensions and a greater transformative edge. All this has produced some fundamental structural and systemic changes in the traditional stratifactory system.[6]

Despite the fact that after India's Independence such qualitative changes had occurred in the stratified system, the changes continued to be interpreted in the old, colonial ideological-valuative frame. The terms and categories used for describing these changes—by the sociologists studying caste as well as by social reformers and political thinkers wanting India to become a caste-less society—were derived from the colonial discourse. This gave rise to two opposite views of change in the caste system, which in fact represented mirror-images of each other. One view, that has long dominated studies on caste in post-Independent India, emphasises certain structural and cultural continuities the Indian society has manifested in the course of modernisation. In this view, changes in caste are seen in terms of functional adjustment made by the system for its own survival and maintenance. The other view, that dominated the political-ideological discourse on caste until recently, sees modernisation as a linear, universal force of history, transforming the caste system into a polarised structure of economic classes. On the whole, the discourse on caste in post-Independent India has remained bogged down in the dichotomous debate on 'tradition' versus 'modernity' and 'caste' versus 'class'.

Secularisation of Caste

The dichotomous view of change has prevented scholars, policy makers and political activists alike, from taking a view of the process by which caste has changed and a new type of stratifactory system has emerged. This process, which can broadly be characterised as secularisation of caste, has detached caste from the ritual status hierarchy on the one hand, and has imparted it a character of the power-group functioning in the competitive democratic politics on the other. Changes in caste thus could be observed along these two dimensions of secularisation: deritualisation and politicisation. These changes have (a) pushed caste out of the traditional stratifactory system, (b) linked it to the new structure of representational power, and (c) in their cumulative impact on caste they have made it possible for individual members of a caste to claim and achieve new economic interest and a class-like identity.

Notes

1. Cohn, Bernard S., "Notes on the History of the Study of Indian Society and Culture", *An Anthropologist among the Historians and Other Essays*, Oxford University Press, Delhi, 1987, pp. 139–40.

2. Cohn (Supra note 1), pp. 141–162.
3. For a detailed discussion on changes in caste under British Rule in India and the impact the colonial policies had on the caste system, see Ghurye, G.S., "Caste During the British Rule" in his *Caste and Race in India,* Popular Prakashan, Bombay, 1962, pp. 270–305. Also see Galanter Marc, "Reform, Mobility, and Politics under British Rule" in his *Competing Equalities: Law and Backward Classes in India,* Oxford University Press, Delhi 1984, pp. 18–40.
4. Collect self-awareness among the lower-caste as a people, oppressed socially and economically by the ritually high ranking castes, developed and found organisational articulation through their participation in anti-Brahman movements which grew in the early decades of this century. See Omvedt, Gail., *Cultural Revolt in a Colonial Society: The Non Brahman Movements in Western India*—1873 to 1930, Scientific Socialist Education Trust, Bombay, 1976. See also F., Irshick, Engene *Politics and Social Conflict in South India: The Non-Brahman Movements and Tamil Separatism 1916–1929,* University of California Press, Berkeley, 1969.
5. Galanter sees this development during the colonial rule as having brought about some important changes in the caste-system: "Caste organisation brought with it two important and related changes in the nature of castes. The salient groups grew in size from endogamous jatis into region-wise alliances. Concomitantly, the traditional patterns of organisation and leadership in the village setting were displaced by voluntary associations with officials whose delimited authority derived from elections." Galanter, (...op.cit.).
6. For a recent argument articulating a contrary position emphasising that the caste system has even in the face of such changes, maintained systemic continuity, see Shah, A.M., "A Response to the Critique on Division and Hierarchy" in Shah, A.M. and Desai, I.P., *Division and Hierarchy: An Overview of Caste in Gujarat,* Hindustan Publishing Corporation, Delhi, 1988, pp. 92–133. Shah sees horizontal divisions as intrinsic to the caste-system itself, representing another principle of caste organisation which has always operated in juxtaposition with 'hierarchy'. The horizontal divisions in caste, in his view, are

thus produced and reproduced as part of the continuous process within the system, a kind of change that a system undergoes for its own survival and maintenance. Whereas for his interlocutor in the debate I.P. Desai, the horizontal divisions which are prior to caste but were integrated in the system of castes by the principle of ritual hierarchy, are now breaking away from that hierarchy and interact in horizontal social and political spaces. In this sense, for Desai, horizontal divisions represent a new principle for the emerging stratificatory system which has undermined the caste principle of ritual hierarchy. Desai, I.P., "A Critique of Division and Hierarchy", in the above cited *Division and Hierarchy*, pp. 40–49.

ANNEXURE 5

(Quoted from R.K. Kshirsagar, *Dalit Movement in India and its Leaders*, M.D. Publications Pvt. Ltd., New Delhi)

The Theory of Taboo

Every caste Hindu believing in the Vedas believes in varnashrama, caste system and caste purity or taboo. It is stated in the Purusha Sukta part of the *Rigveda*, that the Brahmin, Kshatriya, Vaisya and Sudra were created by God respectively from the mouth, arms, thighs and feet. The untouchable, however, were not Savarnas. They were known as avarnas. Hence in the hierarchy of the caste system they were more degraded and treated as outcastes, untouchables, whose touch was considered to be profane.

The *Bhagavad Gita* while narrating the duties of each and every Varna states categorically that "by worshipping through the performance of his own duty (Dharma) man attains perfection." Performing one's own duties or Dharma was, thus, made essential for salvation. Therefore, none could afford to challenge the Dharma revealed in the religious books. Ultimately, the habit of untouchability formed Achar Dharma of all the caste Hindus.

Thus, Hindus have no explanation as to the origin of untouchability. At the most they try to explain it in terms of fictitious belief in caste purity, taboo and inequality of castes. Therefore, the theory of taboo fails to explain the origin of untouchability.

Race and Occupation Theory

Stainly Rice propounded the theory of race and occupation for explaining the origin of untouchability. According to him, the untouchables were non-Aryan and non-Dravidian aboriginals. They were conquered and subjugated by the Dravidians first and thereafter by the Aryans. Accordingly, there were two invasions of India, first by the Dravidians and second by the

Aryans. The Aryans vanquished the non-Aryans, reduced them to mere 'serfs' and assigned to them only menial or filthy occupations. According to Babasaheb Ambedkar, this theory presupposes the homogeneous nature of Aryans, whereas they were divided into Rig-Vedic Aryans and Atharva-Vedic Aryans. The Dravidians were not racially different from the aboriginals. There is no record that the vanquished became untouchables. According to anthropometry test, the untouchables resemble the high caste people; most of the names of *kul* and *gotra* also are identical to those of untouchables. The filthy and unclean occupations which the untouchables performed were common to all human societies but this practice could not come into existence elsewhere.

Multi-causal Theory

According to V.R. Shinde there were five different causes for the origin of untouchability. They were as follows:

1. Those who were living by performing filthy or unclean occupations were treated as untouchables.
2. Those who were independent entities, but later on were vanquished in the wars became untouchables.
3. Those who were Buddhists and non-believers in God, superstitions and Vedas and did not accept the supremacy of Brahmanism were made untouchables.
4. The tribals not living like civilians also came under this category.
5. The marriage of a high caste female with a low caste male was called *Pratiloma* marriage and it was prohibited. Those who performed *Pratiloma* marriage in contravention of the Dharma Shastras were boycotted and discarded as untouchables.

The Broken Men Theory

According to Dr. Babasaheb Ambedkar the untouchables were the Broken Men. The primitive society was mainly tribal. At a later stage they became settled as soon as they switched to agriculture as a means of their livelihood. However, all the tribes did not settle simultaneously. Some tribes were still nomadic while others settled down.

There were intra-tribal wars as well as wars between settled and nomadic tribes. The causes for the intra-tribal warfare were (i) stealing cattle, (ii) stealing women, and (iii) stealthy grazing of cattle in the pastures belonging to others. On the other hand, the causes for the war between settled people and nomadic tribes were (a) the nomads found it more advantageous to fight against the settlers and steal their wealth, and (b) the settlers were unable to defend themselves from the nomads who were naturally more militant and aggressive.

Intra-tribal wars gave rise to divisions among tribes. The defeated tribes were broken into groups. Hence, there always existed in primitive times a floating population constituting groups of Broken Tribesmen. On the other hand, the settled versus nomadic war caused loss of property and lives among the former. They were facing the acute problem of defence from certain aggressive tribes. Thus the Broken Men were in need of shelter and food whereas the settled were in need of protection of the property and persons. Consequently, they had to come to a certain settlement and form an agreement for protecting each other's interests. "Although we have," he states, "no written text of contract coming down to us from antiquity we can say that the two struck a bargain whereby the Broken Men agreed to do the work of watch and ward for the settled tribes and the settled tribes agreed to give them food and shelter. Indeed it would have been unnatural if such an agreement had not been made between the two especially when the interests of the one required the co-operation of the other."

The primitive settlers, however, were not so liberal as to admit the alien into their area, hence they allotted the land outside the village to the nomadic tribes. From the protection or strategic point of view, their settlement outside the village was necessary so as to face the prospective dangers. Obviously, because of their living outside the village they were called Antyaja or Antyavasin.

The second reason for the origin of untouchability according to Dr. Babasaheb Ambedkar was the contempt for Buddhism, the religion professed by the Broken Men. The Broken Men who were segregated from the village people must have been inclined to embrace Buddhism which was based on liberty, equality and fraternity. The village people who remained in the Hindu fold accepted the supremacy of the Brahmins, whereas the broken men discarded the supremacy of the latter and continued to prefer Buddhism. This caused strife between the two communities which ended in suppression of the Broken Men and downfall of Buddhism in the later period.

According to Dr. Babasaheb Ambedkar, the third reason for the origin of untouchability was the habit of beef eating by the Broken Men. The untouchable became habituated to eating flesh of cows whereas the touchable gave up the same. Even at the later stage the Brahmins not only gave up this diet, but became purely vegetarian so as to outsmart the Buddhists professing the principle of non-violence and compassion to all men and animals. "Unfortunately, beef eating instead of being treated as a purely secular matter, was made a matter of religion. This happened because the Brahmins made the cow a sacred animal. The Broken Men being guilty of sacrilege necessarily came beyond the pale of society." Thus according to Dr. Babasaheb Ambedkar the 'stain' of untouchability was imposed on these people who were Broken Men, Buddhists and beef eaters.

ANNEXURE 6

(Quoted from M.K. Baruah, *Portrait of a Gandhian: Biography of Dr. Martin King Jr.*, Gauhati, 1985)

Hegel and Walter Rauschenbusch impressed King the most. Hegel's analysis of dialectical process and of the progress of growth through struggle and pain left an indelible imprint on King's mind. According to Hegel's theory world-historical individuals were the agents by which the will of 'universal reason' (the world spirit) is carried out. Hegel said that "an individual if living by itself, and exercising its own caprice, is not free. Only as he blends himself with the group, does he attain true freedom." Hegel held that "history has been striving throughout time towards realisation of a perfect state—a state in which each member so blends himself with the whole, so that will of the whole is his will." King began to question Hegel's contention that universal reason reaches its height in a society of free individuals, each subordinating the individual reason to the universal reason. Speaking of the emergence of 'world-historical individuals,' Hegel said:

> They may all be called Heroes inasmuch as they have derived their purposes and their vocation, not from the calm regular course of things, sanctioned by the existing order; but from a concealed fount, from that inner Spirit, still hidden beneath the surface, which impinges on the outer world as on a shell and bursts into pieces. (Such were Alexander, Caesar, Napoleon.) They were practical, political men. But at the same time they were thinking men who had an insight into the requirement of the time— what was ripe for development. This was the very truth for their age, for their world.... It was theirs to know this nascent principle, the necessary, directly sequent step in progress, which their world was to take; to make this their aim, and to expend their energy in promoting it. World-historical men—the Heroes of an epoch—must therefore be recognised as its clear-sighted ones: their deeds, their words, are the best of their time.[1]

Hegel's words perhaps impressed this young scholar from Atlanta at first, but soon he realised that a man truly concerned about humanity will not wait for the time to come to speak out against social evils and then lead people towards progress. Gandhi did not wait for the right time to come. He was just born on the scene and tried to carry reform from there without waiting for time. There was no doubt that the spirit of the time helped to further his cause, but as a true reformer and a leader of men, Gandhi perhaps could not sit tight waiting for the 'right' time. King could not accept Hegelian philosophy word for word and he held certain reservations about it. However, the study of Hegel helped King towards an understanding of some of the underlying causes of social evils and to see that growth comes through struggle. Hegel's contention that "truth is the whole" led King to reflect on any question with a rational-philosophical argument. Hegel gave this questioning student much food for thought and King's study of Hegel continued until the days of his graduate studies at Boston University.

The second man—one of the most influential in King's life—was Dr. Walter Rauschenbusch, a religious reformer of America. King was familiar with Dr. Rauschenbusch's work since his senior year at Morehouse. Rauschenbusch advocated application of Christian principles to the social problems of his day. As a man who was going to be a minister of the social problems of the Gospel, King realised that he could not dissociate himself from the social problems of the day—particularly those he would be required to face in the future. Describing how he first became aware of social problems, Dr. Rauschenbusch said in his book, *Origin of Social Crisis*

> It did not come from church. It came through personal contact with poverty, and when I saw how men toiled all their life long, and at the end had almost nothing to show for it; how strong men begged for work and could not get it in

> hard times, ... how little children died, ... why, a single human accident of that sort is enough to set a great beacon fire burning to light up the whole world for you, if you only have the right mind in you.

The work of this great reformer, Walter Rauschenbusch kindled the spirit and mind of young King and set the fire burning. King's mind was right, because he was concerned about the poor people who were discriminated because of the colour of their skin, who were robbed of their basic rights, and who were being exploited in affluent America day after day. From his young days in Atlanta, King saw with his own eyes that hundreds of healthy strong Negroes were being displaced from their jobs due to increased mechanisation in the Southern farms. Unable to find jobs in the cities of the South, these poor farmers migrated to the cities of the North, only to discover that the Northern cities were already overcrowded by succeeding waves of migration from the South. Once again, they faced the problem of unemployment. They overcrowded the Northern ghettos. Seeing the plight of these poor impoverished people, King began to reflect on the causes of such social problems. He could clearly see how year after year the poor Negroes were exploited by the whites and how they had suffered for centuries in racist America. While he was a student at Morehouse, King held two different menial jobs in two summers, and since then, he had been aware of the plight of the poor Negroes by his contact with such underprivileged and underpaid people. After his Northern experience, King could see the real suffering of the people who migrated to these overcrowded Northern cities. This experience in the North was also an education for him. The overcrowded ghettos of Washington, Philadelphia and New York furnished him with practical knowledge. While the seminary at Crozer deepened the foundations of the theoretical knowledge that he had already acquired at Morehouse, his study of Rauschenbusch further encouraged him in his search for social cures.

In his book *Fundamental of Social Principles of Jesus*, Rauschenbusch, discussing the value of life, said:

> Christian sense of worth and sacredness of human life has been a greater stabiliser of civil liberty. Reverence of personality is the ruling principle of ethics and religion. It constitutes, therefore, the trust and the highest test either of religion or of civilisation, not to inflict bodily or spiritual injury... The deeper our insight into human destiny becomes, the more sacred does every human seem to us.

Rauschenbusch stressed the natural respect for human life and personality believing that only through reverence for human life can brotherhood and solidarity of mankind be achieved. According to him, love as a social instinct should be the main binding force of such solidarity and understanding; goodwill and forgiveness are absolutely necessary to preserve such unity. He said that in order to achieve this unity, man must overcome the evil instincts of human nature and turn his mind towards the divine. To Rauschenbusch this constitutes the fundamental principles of life.

The study of Rauschenbusch gave young King a broad theological basis for his understanding of those social problems of which he had been aware since his days in Morehouse. Rauschenbusch's gospel dealt with the whole man—not only his soul but also his body; not only his spiritual well-being but also his material well-being. King, then studying to be a minister, was always concerned for the well-being of fellow Negroes and their social and economic conditions, and he, as such, found a natural ally in Rauschenbusch.

Although the study of Rauschenbusch's work helped King to understand the roots of certain social problems, King's questioning mind did not agree with some of the views of the great reformer. Rauschenbusch, like other nineteenth century religious men, believed that human progress is inevitable. King thought that Rauschenbusch was very optimistic about human nature. According to King, Rauschenbusch also came very close to "identifying the kingdom of God with a particular social, economical system." King did not believe that the church should be identified in such a manner with these systems.

Besides Hegel and Rauschenbusch, King studied other social, ethical and political philosophers during the years in Crozer. They were: Socrates, Plato, Aristotle, Rousseau, Bentham, Mill and Locke. All these philosophers stimulated his thinking. He probed deep into the works of each of the above philosophers with a questioning mind. Sometimes, he found himself in agreement with their views and sometimes he did not; but, nevertheless, all their divergent views laid the foundation of an emerging personal philosophy of his own... King admired Socrates because of the thinker's courage to stand up for truth. To Socrates, truth was greater than life. Socrates asked time and time again: "What is good?" His answer was: "Knowledge is the highest good." Socrates thought that no man is voluntarily bad and that through knowledge one knows what is good, and he will choose to do that thing. According to Socrates, life is always inquiring and trying to discover what is good is order to make it worth living. To Plato, goodness is tied to the nature of the universe, "The world of sense," he thought, "is unreal, fleeting and changing." To him this is evil. He said that the real world of pure unchanging ideas is the world of good and man can know this real world only through reason. According to him, reason is the highest good for man and the goal of life is the release of the soul from the body so that it can contemplate the true world of ideas. Plato said that man's life consists of three parts: body—functional part; the spiritual part—courage and bravery; and reason—the highest part of man. A man lives a good life when reason rules his will and appetite. Then, he is wise, brave and temperate. Thus a life of reason is the highest good for man. According to Plato, a life of wisdom, courage and self control, is the only kind of happy life. One should not seek pleasure as the only aim of life.

Aristotle pointed out that every action of man has some end in view and this chain seems to be an endless chain. One acts in order to get something, but that something again is obtained to get something else, and so on. Besides each being is different from the other, each having his own talents and abilities. What, he asked, is the highest good—the good for which all else is done. That good is the full realisation of the talents and abilities inherent in every being. Thus self-realisation, is for Aristotle, the highest good—the goal for which all else is done. No other entity possesses reason as man. Therefore the highest good is the complete realisation of reason which brings happiness.

But reason, as Aristotle thought, is only a part of man. He also has feelings, appetites and desires. A good life is one in which all these factors are realised in perfect harmony, in which reason rules and the feelings and desires obey.

Therefore, the goal of human life is to have rational attitude towards feelings and desires, in other words, a balanced life.

John Stuart Mill contended that the measure of goodness should be in terms of "the greatest good for the greatest number." This eliminates selfishness. Jeremy Bentham, though he believed as Mill did in terms of the "greatest good for the greatest number," only justified this position on the basis of self-interest, holding that to so act, will actually bring the greatest good only to the one acting.

King was stimulated by the reading of Plato and Aristotle's rule of reason and Mill's and Bentham's philosophy of reforms in building up a more ideal society. King was in agreement with Mill that social well-being is necessary for individual well-being as the individual is tied up with the group and his happiness is dependent upon the status of the group. Like Mill, King began to dream of a great American society where happiness and prosperity for all are certain and where all the people would share the wealth of this affluent society. King began to reflect on the conditions of black people in American society. He could clearly see that in order to improve the individual well-being of black Americans, it would be necessary to think in terms of black people as a whole. He concluded that it would be impossible to improve their individual economic status if certain collective action was not taken to that end. To him, it was only through the improved status of the black people as a whole that the individual black could be really happy.

In Thomas Hobbes' theory of social contract, people surrender their right to rule in order to preserve others. Hobbes believed that absolute monarchy was the best form of government and that the king was God's representative on earth and God spoke through him. Freedom of religion would not be tolerated. The religion of the king would have to be that of the people. Locke was in complete disagreement with Hobbes who believed that the natural state of man is one of war and self-seeking. To Locke, the original state of all men was one of perfect freedom and equality. Since all men were free and equal, no one had the right to take away another's life, liberty, possessions. To Locke, the structure of society was established by social contract agreed upon by the members of the group. Each member was obliged to submit to the authority of the majority. This was necessary for efficient living together since unanimous consent was next to impossible in a large group.

Note

1. Bennet, Larone, *What Manner of Man: A Biography of Dr. Martin Luther King*, p. 28.

ANNEXURE 7

Ambedkar regarded Dhamma as religion. He observed, "Religion is personal, contrary to this, Dhamma is social." He described Dhamma as righteousness, right relations between man and man in all spheres of life. The Buddhist way of life aimed at the moral regeneration and social emancipation of all human beings. According to him, there were only four preceptors—Shri Krishna, Buddha, Christ and Mohammed. Buddha appealed to him most as he always preached that his disciples should not obey his commands but should follow the dictates of their conscience. There is no god in Buddhism, but the place of god is taken by morality.

The merits of Buddhist philosophy are given as follows: (a) Buddhism demands living existence and a life divine attainable here and now—and not after death. (b) It is a realism—never an idealism. (c) It upholds liberty, equality, truth and justice—it pours on humanity love and peace. (d) It is dynamic, scientific and all-embracing. (e) Its explanation of life and its meaning and purpose of birth and its nature, of death and its aftermath is very clear, intelligible and logical. (f) Above all, man is the centre of its study and examination, not anything outside him. On the contrary, the static nature of Hindu Dharma and society was emphasised as below: (a) Hindu society is as it was in B.C. with trivial modifications. (b) Untouchability is recognised by the Hindu religion; it is deeply rooted in Hindu society. (c) Caste is the corner-stone to the arch of Hinduism.[1]

According to Ambedkar, Hinduism and Buddhism differed in three vital aspects. In Hindu religion, there is Ishwar (God), Atma (soul), and Varna system; in Buddhism, there is no Ishwar, soul and caste or Varna system.

Ambedkar was always of the view that social and human reconstruction needed a religious basis.[2] In a speech on the British Broadcasting Corporation he outlined his preference of Buddhism to Hinduism. He preferred Buddhism because it gave three principles in combination which no other religion gave: Buddhism teaches Prajna (understanding against superstition and supernaturalism), Karuna (love), and Samata (equality). He preferred Buddhism because like Christianity it afforded hope to the downtrodden.[3]

According to him, Buddhism was a true religion because it led to a life guided by the three principles of knowledge, right path and compassion. He remarked, "Buddhism is a part and parcel of Bharatiya culture. I have taken care that my conversion will not harm the tradition of the culture and history of this land."[4] He said in an interview on 13 October 1956 at Nagpur that he would not remain a member of the S.C.F. after conversion to Buddhism. There were two mottos before him "buddham sharanam gachhami" which means "I am surrendering myself to the person possessed of knowledge"; and the other is "sangam saranam gachhami" i.e., "I am surrendering myself to Sanghs—Guilds". Sangh means social life: to him Buddha was a great socialist of his times. He was a rationalist and he rooted out the monopoly of Brahmins.[5]

Notes

1. Deva and Wagh, *Dr. Ambedkar's Conversion,* pp. 4–5
2. Ibid., pp. 19–24.
3. Ambedkar's Speeches, vol. II, p. 115
4. Keer, op. cit., p. 495.
5. Mahanirvan, special number, p. 17.

ANNEXURE 8
(Quoted from M.K. Baruah, *Portrait of a Gandhi: Biography of Dr. Martin King Jr.*, Gauhati, 1985)

Like Frederick Douglass, the unofficial President of the black people of America in the years before and immediately after the civil war whose achievements made the careers of other people seem puny, King was concerned with the universal struggle for the freedom of people everywhere, irrespective of the colour of their skin. Frederick once said, "We are not all the same and every one of us joins the fight to further human brotherhood." Douglass was a slave and lifted himself up from the bondage of slavery and also tried to unmask others from this cruel veil. Like Douglass, Dr. King tried to lift his people from the perpetual state of frustration, which resulted from centuries of exploitation, to dignity, faith and hope. Dr. King was concerned not only with desegregation but, like Douglass, he proposed reforms for them. In a speech at the Higham Anti-slavery Convention in November 1841, Douglass exclaimed.

> We ought to do what the slave-holders do not want us to do, that is, use moral suasion. They care nothing about political action; they don't dread the political movement. It is the moral movement, the appeal to men's sense of right, which makes them and all our opponents tremble.

Douglass believed that 'moral suasion' would succeed in changing the mind of the entire nation including the slave-holders. Like Douglass, King believed that the 'moral suasion' was necessary to change the minds of racists. According to him such change could be achieved by the power of 'love'. He used to preach to his followers:

> We shall match your capacity to inflict suffering by our capacity to endure suffering. We shall meet your physical force with soul force. Do to us what you will, and we shall

> continue to love you. We cannot in all good conscience obey your unjust laws, because non-cooperation with evil is as much a moral obligation as is cooperation with good. Throw us in jail, and we shall still love you. Bomb our homes and threaten our children, and we shall still love you. Send your hooded perpetrators of violence into our community at the midnight hour and beat us and leave us half dead, and we shall still love you. But be ye assured that we will wear you down by our capacity to surrender. One day we shall win freedom, but not only for ourselves. We shall so appeal to your heart and conscience that we shall win you in the process, and our victory will be a double victory.

Douglass' emphasis was on 'moral suasion,' or moral reasoning in place of the 'militant abolitionism'. King also emphasised non-violence or 'Satyagraha' as opposed to violence advocated by the militant members of the 'black power' movement. King believed that by obtaining political power the blacks could themselves improve their economic conditions. Like Douglass, King tried to appeal to noble qualities of the white power structure. He never tried to coerce...

King was the first major leader since the days of Booker T. Washington based in the south. He did not draw talent or resources from labour unions or political groups. On the contrary, King identified with both the Negro church and the Negro masses. Like Washington he was also concerned with economic uplift of his people. Washington did not stress obtaining political power for the Negroes; instead, he emphasised on the economic power. Perhaps, Washington's policy was pragmatic for his time. Booker T. Washington's goals were to achieve unqualified integration in American society, but he was pragmatic and realised that the blacks could do little at that time to block the current of discrimination. He had to put up with it only by emphasising reforms where it was practical and possible.

Observing the objective quality of Washington's leadership, his biographer, Samuel R. Spenser, remarked:

> He was like a seasoned boxer. He never took the full force of his opponent's attack, but rolled with the punch, attempting to protect himself and his race for the most effective battles later.

Perhaps, Mr. Spenser is right. Had Washington taken a policy advocating desegregation and the Negro franchise at that time, he surely would have alienated the white power structure on whom the Negroes economically were dependent at that time. In that case, he would not perhaps have achieved the economic gain for the blacks as much as he did...

Washington argued that economic progress could only offer a means of full integration. It was no less important than political means. To him, both were complementary. Furthermore, by infusing in his people certain qualities, hardwork, thrift and initiative by his industrial education, he wanted to give them certain pride, dignity and economic security. Washington thought that such things would eventually make integration easier.

He perhaps thought that he could accomplish more by telling the white men what they wanted to hear. Washington mostly emphasised economic freedom as a prelude to political freedom. He perhaps did whatever he thought was best, whatever was practicable in that time.

King, on the contrary, emphasised immediate integration of blacks in American society while at the same time he was thinking about the economic uplift of the people. Dr. King said, "Our ultimate goal is integration which is genuine intergroup and interpersonal living." Washington was silent on this idea. "I have never at anytime asked or expected that anyone, in dealing with me, should overlook or forget that I am Negro," said Washington. He himself was completely free from racial prejudice and lifted himself above the level of hatred and prejudice. Washington said late in his life, "We must learn to think not in terms of race or colour or language or religion or political boundaries, but in terms of humanity."

Like Washington Dr. King was completely free from racial prejudice and personal ambition. King possessed the genuine humility of Washington and identified himself with the common man. Like Washington, King asked all Americans not to think in terms of race or colour, but in terms of human brotherhood. To both, the colour of skin had nothing to do with his potential contribution to society. Washington wanted to achieve equality for the blacks by patient plea and persuasion. King however thought that "pressureless persuasion of Booker T. Washington only served as a springboard for the racist southerner to drive into deeper and more ruthless oppression of Negroes." As opposed to Washington, Dr. King believed that the Negroes must gain political rights in order to gain all possible economic advancement. That was the reason he insisted on Negros' right to vote throughout the South and risked his life many times for that purpose. However, Dr King refused to label Booker T. Washington as 'Uncle Tom' as many militant leaders and some of Washington's critics did. Sympathising with Booker T. Washington's position, Dr. King wrote:

> I do not share the notion that he was an Uncle Tom who compromised for the sake of keeping the peace. Washington sincerely believed that if the South was not forced to do something that it did not for the moment want to do, it would voluntarily rally in the end to the Negro's cause. Washington's error was that he underestimated the structures of evil; as a consequence his philosophy of pressureless persuasion only served as a springboard for racist Southerners to drive into deeper and more ruthless oppression of the Negro.

William Edward Burghardt Du Bois, a professor of history at Atlanta University, another Negro leader, was a severe critic of Washington. Eight years after Booker T. Washington's Atlanta speech, he published a little book of essays, which he named, *The Soul of Black Folks.* The book described how it felt to be a Negro at the beginning of the 20th century. "One ever feels his twoness," Du Bois wrote. "An American, a Negro; two worlds, two thoughts, two warring ideals in one dark body whose dogged strength alone keeps it from being torn asunder." In that book he talked about the Negro's tragic past. With the passion of a poet, he saw a future—a hope—perhaps a dream for his time. He looked forward to the day when men would ask not, "Is he white?" but "Can he work?" In his book, *The Soul of Black Folks,* Du Bois included an essay entitled "Of Mr. Booker T. Washington" in which he described Washington as "the most distinguished Southerner since Jefferson Davis," though he thought that Washington's Atlanta Compromise was wrong. He pointed out that life for Negroes in the South was growing worse each day.

Du Bois became more convinced that a new type of Negro leadership was needed. In 1905, he called a conference of men interested in "organised, determined and aggressive action." A group of teachers, ministers and businessmen met in Niagara Falls (on the Canadian side, because no hotel in the United States would rent them a room) to form Niagara Movement...

Dr. Du Bois became the leader of one section of the black people that opposed Booker T. Washington. In 1910, the Niagara Movement merged with other groups to form the NAACP and Du Bois became its Director of Publications and Research. Du Bois thought that Washington's view of society was too limited and his remedies to overcome the ills of the Negroes were insufficient, if not positively harmful.

But Du Bois was not a born leader of men like Booker T. Washington and Dr. King. He was not at home in the crowd. He read speeches in a crisp, cultivated voice, with no gestures and jokes; witty and warm in small groups, yet he was shy in public. However, Du Bois was an articulate protestor on behalf of the blacks. Both Du Bois and King viewed the Negro problem as a national problem but to Washington, it was only a problem for the Negro himself. Both King and Du Bois insisted on Negroes' right to vote, civil equality and equal facilities for education. Both men were willing to fight for the principles even if it meant sacrifice of life. King was religious, whereas Du Bois was romantic and intellectual. King was spiritual linked to the Divine; Du Bois was poetic and emotional, and was linked to ideas. In contrast to Du Bois' poetic temperament, King was of a temperament that was simple, direct, prosaic and serene. King possessed genuine humility and like Washington, he had the ability to identify with the common people. Du Bois was impenetrable, eccentric and aloof. King's faith in man and in god were somewhat ingenuous. Du Bois thought that the Southern white men were enemies of the black people. To King, they were not enemies, but the racism was the enemy. Du Bois did not think that average Southern white men had any desire to help the blacks. He did not see any future for young blacks in the South. He encouraged them to go to the Northern cities.

On the contrary, Dr. King himself went back to the South to serve his people and to lead them to freedom and equality. He thought that there were many Southern white men who were really friends of the black people.

ANNEXURE 9

(Quoted from *Strides Toward Freedom (1958)* by Martin Luther King Jr. as given in *Black Writers of America*, The Macmillan Company, New York, 1972)

IV: The Day of Days, December 5

My wife and I awoke earlier than usual on Monday morning. We were up and fully dressed by five-thirty. The day for the protest had arrived, and we were determined to see the first act of this unfolding drama. I was still saying that if we could get 60 per cent cooperation the venture would be a success.

Fortunately, a bus stop was just five feet from our house. This meant that we could observe the opening stages from our front window. The first bus was to pass around six o'clock. And so we waited through an interminable half hour. I was in the kitchen drinking my coffee when I heard Coretta cry, "Martin, Martin, come quickly!" I put down my cup and ran toward the living room. As I approached the front window Coretta pointed joyfully to a slowly moving bus: "Darling, it is empty!" I could hardly believe what I saw. I knew that the South Jackson line, which ran past our house, carried more Negro passengers than any other line in Montgomery, and that this first bus was usually filled with domestic workers going to their jobs. Would all of the other buses follow the pattern that had been set by the first? Eagerly we waited for the next bus. In fifteen minutes it rolled down the street, and, like the first, it was empty. A third bus appeared, and it too was empty of all but two white passengers.

I jumped in my car and for almost an hour I cruised down every major street and examined every passing bus. During this hour, at the peak of the morning traffic, I saw no more than eight Negro passengers riding the buses. By this time I was jubilant. Instead of the 60 per cent cooperation we had hoped for, it was becoming apparent that we had reached almost 100 per cent. A miracle had taken place. The once dormant and quiescent Negro community was now fully awake.

All day long it continued. At the afternoon peak the buses were still as empty of Negro passengers as they had been in the morning. Students of Alabama State College, who usually kept the South Jackson bus crowded, were cheerfully walking or thumbing rides. Job holders had either found other means of transportation or made their way on foot. While some rode in cabs or private cars, others used less conventional means. Men were seen riding mules to work, and more than one horse-drawn buggy drove on the streets of Montgomery that day.

During the rush hours the sidewalks were crowded with laborers and domestic workers, many of them well past middle age, trudging patiently to their jobs and home again, sometimes as much as twelve miles. They knew why they walked, and the knowledge was evident in the way they carried themselves. And as I watched them I knew that there is nothing more majestic than the determined courage of individuals willing to suffer and sacrifice for their freedom and dignity.

Many spectators had gathered at the bus stops to watch what was happening. At first they stood quietly, but as the day progressed they began to cheer the empty buses and laugh and make jokes. Noisy youngsters could be heard singing out, "No riders today." Trailing each bus through the Negro section were two policemen on motorcycles, assigned by the city commissioners, who claimed that Negro "goon squads" had been organised to keep other Negroes from riding the buses. In the course of the day the police succeeded in making one arrest. A college student who was helping an elderly woman across the street was charged with "intimidating passengers." But the "goon squads" existed only in the commission's imagination. No one was threatened or intimidated for riding the buses; the only harassment anyone faced was that of his own conscience.

Around nine-thirty in the morning I tore myself from the action of the city streets and headed for the crowded police court. Here Mrs. Parks was being tried for disobeying the city segregation ordinance. Her attorney, Fred D. Grey—the brilliant young Negro who later became the chief counsel for the protest movement—was on hand to defend her. After the judge heard the arguments, he found Mrs. Parks guilty and fined her ten dollars and court costs (a total of fourteen dollars). She appealed the case. This was one of the first clear-cut instances in which a Negro had been convicted for disobeying the segregation law. In the past, either cases like this had been dismissed or the people involved had been charged with disorderly conduct. So in a real sense the arrest and conviction of Mrs. Parks had a twofold impact: it was a precipitating factor to arouse the Negroes to positive action and it was a test of the validity of the segregation law itself. I am sure that supporters of such prosecuton would have acted otherwise if they had the presence to look beyond the moment.

Leaving Mrs. Parks' trial, Ralph Abernathy, E.D. Nixon, and Rev. E.N. French—then minister of the Hilliard Chapel A.M.E. Zion Church—discussed the need for some organisation to guide and direct the protest. Up to this time things had moved forward more or less spontaneously. These men were wise enough to see that the moment had now come for a clearer order and direction.

Meanwhile Roy Bennett had called several people together at three o'clock to make plans for the evening mass meeting. Everyone present was elated by the tremendous success that had already attended the protest. But beneath this feeling was the question, where do we go from here? When E.D. Nixon reported on his discussion with Abernathy and French earlier in the day, and their suggestions for an ad hoc organisation, the group responded enthusiastically. The next job was to elect the officers for the new organisation.

As soon as Bennett had opened the nominations for president, Rufus Lewis spoke from the far corner of the room: "Mr. Chairman, I would like to nominate Reverend M.L. King for president." The motion was seconded and carried, and in a matter of minutes I was unanimously elected.

The action had caught me unawares. It had happened so quickly that I did not even have time to think it through. It is probable that if I had, I would have declined the nomination. Just three weeks before, several members of the local chapter of the NAACP had urged me to run for the presidency of that organisation, assuring me that I was certain of election. After my wife and I had discussed the matter, we agreed that I should not then take on any heavy community responsibilities, since I had so recently finished my thesis, and needed to give more attention to my church work. But on this occasion events had moved too fast.

The election of the remaining officers was speedily completed: Rev. L. Roy Bennett, vice-president; Rev. U.J. Fields, recording secretary; Rev. E.N. French, corresponding secretary; Mrs. Erna A. Dungee, financial secretary; Mr. E.D. Nixon, treasurer. It was then agreed that all those present would constitute the executive board of the new organisation. This board would serve as the coordinating agency of the whole movement. It was a well-balanced group, including ministers of all denominations, school teachers, businessmen, and two lawyers.

The new organisation needed a name, and several were suggested. Someone proposed the Negro Citizens Committee; but this was rejected because it resembled too closely the White Citizens Council. Other suggestions were made and dismissed until finally Ralph Abernathy offered a name that was agreeable to all—the Montgomery Improvement Association (MIA).

With these organisational matters behind us, we turned to a discussion of the evening meeting. Several people, not wanting the reporters to know our future moves, suggested that we just sing and pray; if there were specific recommendations to be made to the people, these could be mimeographed and passed out secretly during the meeting. This, they felt, would leave the reporters in the dark. Others urged that something should be done to conceal the true identity of the leaders, feeling that if no particular name was revealed it would be safer for all involved. After a rather lengthy discussion, E.D. Nixon rose impatiently "We are acting like little boys," he said.

> Somebody's name will have to be known, and if we are afraid we might just as well fold up right now. We must also be men enough to discuss our recommendations in the open: this idea of secretly passing something around on paper is a lot of bunk. The white folk are eventually going to find it out anyway. We'd better decide now if we are going to be fearless men or scared boys.

With this forthright statement the air was cleared. Nobody would again suggest that we try to conceal our identity or avoid facing the issue head on. Nixon's courageous affirmation had given new heart to those who were about to be crippled by fear.

It was unanimously agreed that the protest should continue until certain demands were met, and that a committee under the chairmanship of Ralph Abernathy would draw up these demands in the form of a resolution and present them to the evening mass meeting for approval. We worked out the remainder of the program quickly. Bennett would preside and I would make the main address. Remarks by a few other speakers, along with scripture reading, prayer, hymns and collection, would round out the program.

Immediately the resolution committee set to drafting its statement. Despite the success of the protest so far, we were still concerned. Would the evening meeting be well attended? Could we hope that the fortitude and enthusiasm of the Negro community would survive more than one such day of hardship? Someone suggested that perhaps we should reconsider our decision to continue the protest. "Would it not be better, said the speaker,

> to call off the protest while it is still a success rather than let it go on a few more days and fizzle out? We have already proved our united strength to the white community. It we stop now we can get anything we want from the bus company simply because they will have the feeling that we can do it again. But if we continue, and most of the people return to the buses tomorrow or the next day, the white people will laugh at us, and we will end up getting nothing.

This argument was so convincing that we almost resolved to end the protest. But we finally agreed to let the mass meeting—which was only about an hour off—be our guide. If the meeting was well attended and the people were enthusiastic, we would continue; otherwise we would call off the protest that night.

I went home for the first time since seven that morning, and found Coretta relaxing from a long day of telephone calls and general excitement. After we had brought each other up to date on the day's developments, I told her, somewhat hesitantly—not knowing what her reaction would be—that I had been elected president of the new association. I need not have worried. Naturally surprised, she still saw that since the responsibility had fallen on me, I had no alternative but to accept it. She did not need to be told that we would now have even less time together, and she seemed undisturbed at the possible danger to all of us in my new position. "You know," she said quietly, "that whatever you do, you have my backing."

Reassured, I went to my study and closed the door. The minutes were passing fast. It was now six-thirty, and I had to leave no later than six-fifty to get to the meeting. This meant that I had only twenty minutes to prepare the most decisive speech of my life. As I thought of the limited time before me and the possible implications of this speech, I became possessed by fear. Each week I needed at least fifteen hours to prepare my Sunday sermon. Now I was faced with the inescapable task of preparing, in almost no time at all, a speech that was expected to give a sense of direction to a people imputed with a new and still unplumbed passion for justice. I was also conscious that reporters and television men would be there with their pencils and sound cameras poised to record my words and send them across the nation.

I was now almost overcome, obsessed by a feeling of inadequacy. In this state of anxiety, I had already wasted five minutes of the original twenty. With nothing left but faith in a power whose matchless strength stands over against the frailties and inadequacies of human nature, I turned to God in prayer. My words were brief and simple, asking God to restore my balance and to be with me in a time when I needed his guidance more than ever.

With less than fifteen minutes left, I began preparing an outline. In the midst of this, however, I faced a new and sobering dilemma: How could I make a speech that would be militant enough to keep my people aroused to positive action and yet moderate enough to keep this fervor within controllable and Christian bounds? I knew that many of the Negro people were victims of bitterness that could easily rise to flood proportions. What could I say to keep them courageous and prepared for positive action and yet devoid of hate and resentment? Could the militant and the moderate be combined in a single speech?

I decided that I had to face the challenge head on, and attempt to combine two apparent irreconcilables. I would seek to arouse the group to action by insisting that their self-respect was at stake and that if they accepted such injustices without protesting, they would betray their own sense of dignity and the eternal edicts of God Himself. But I would balance this with a strong affirmation of the Christian doctrine of love. By the time I had sketched an outline of the speech in my mind, my time was up. Without stopping to eat supper (I had not eaten since morning) I said good-bye to Coretta and drove to the Holt Street Church.

Within five blocks of the church I noticed a traffic jam. Cars were lined up as far as I could see on both sides of the street. It was a moment before it occurred to me that all of these cars were headed for the mass meeting. I had to park at least four blocks from the church, and as I started walking I noticed that hundreds of people were standing outside. In the dark night, police cars circled slowly around the area, surveying the orderly, patient, and good-humored crowd. The three or four thousand people who could not get into the church were to stand cheerfully throughout the evening listening to the proceedings on the loudspeakers that had been set up outside for their benefit. And when, near the end of the meeting, these speakers were silenced at the request of the white people in surrounding neighborhoods, the crowd would still remain quietly, content simply to be present.

It took fully fifteen minutes to push my way through to the pastor's study, where Dr. Wilson told me that the church had been packed since five o'clock. By now my doubts concerning the continued success of our venture were dispelled. The question of calling off the protest was now academic. The enthusiasm of these thousands of people swept everything along like an onrushing tidal wave.

It was some time before the remaining speakers could push their way to the rostrum through the tightly packed church. When the meeting began it was almost half an hour late. The opening hymn was the old familiar "Onward, Christian Soldiers," and when that mammoth audience stood to sing, the voices outside swelling the chorus in the church, there was a mighty ring like the glad echo of heaven itself.

Rev. W.F. Alford, minister of the Beulah Baptist Church, led the congregation in prayer, followed by a reading of the

Scripture by Rev. U.J. Fields, minister of the Bell Street Baptist Church. Then the chairman introduced me. As the audience applauded, I rose and stood before the pulpit. Television cameras began to shoot from all sides. The crowd grew quiet.

Without manuscript or notes, I told the story of what had happened to Mrs. Parks. Then I reviewed the long history of abuses and insults that Negro citizens had experienced on the city buses. "But there comes a time," I said, "when people get tired".

> We are here this evening to say to those who have mistreated us so long that we are tired—tired of being segregated and humiliated; tired of being kicked about by the brutal feet of oppression.

The congregation met this statement with fervent applause. "We had no alternative but to protest," I continued,

> For many years, we have shown amazing patience. We have sometimes given our white brothers the feeling that we liked the way we were being treated. But we come here tonight to be saved from that patience that makes us patient with anything less than freedom and justice.

Again the audience interrupted with applause.

Briefly I justified our actions, both morally and legally. "One of the great glories of democracy is the right to protest for right." Comparing our methods with those of the White Citizens Councils and the Ku Klux Klan, I pointed out that while these organisations are protesting for the perpetuation of injustice in the community, we are protesting for the birth of justice in the community. Their methods lead to violence and lawlessness. But in our protest there will be no cross burnings. No white person will be taken from his home by a hooded Negro mob and brutally murdered. There will be no threats and intimidation. We will be guided by the highest principles of law and order.

With this groundwork for militant action, I moved on to words of caution. I urged the people not to force anybody to refrain from riding the buses.

> Our method will be that of persuasion, not coercion. We will only say to the people, "Let your conscience be your guide." Emphasising the Christian doctrine of love, our actions must be guided by the deepest principles of our Christian faith. Love must be our regulating ideal. Once again we must hear the words of Jesus echoing across the centuries: "Love your enemies, bless them that curse you, and pray for them that despitefully use you." If we fail to do this our protest will end up as a meaningless drama on the stage of history, and its memory will be shrouded with the ugly garments of shame. In spite of the mistreatment that we have confronted we must not become bitter, and end up by hating our white brothers. As Booker T. Washington said, "Let no man pull you so low as to make you hate him."

Once more the audience responded enthusiastically. Then came my closing statement.

> If you will protest courageously, and yet with dignity and Christian love, when the history books are written in future generations, the historians will have to pause and say, "There lived a great people—a black people—who injected new meaning and dignity into the veins of civilisation." This is our challenge and our overwhelming responsibility.

As I took my seat the people rose to their feet and applauded. I was thankful to God that the message had gotten over and that the task of combining the militant and the moderate had been at least partially accomplished. The people had been as enthusiastic when I urged them to love as they were when I urged them to protest.

As I sat listening to the continued applause I realised that this speech had evoked more response than any speech or sermon I had ever delivered, and yet it was virtually unprepared. I came to see for the first time what the older preachers meant when they said, "Open your mouth and God will speak for you." While I would not let this experience tempt me to overlook the need for continued preparation, it would always remind me that God can transform man's weakness into his glorious opportunity.

When Mrs. Parks was introduced from the rostrum by E.N. French, the audience responded by giving her a standing ovation. She was their heroine. They saw in her courageous person the symbol of their hopes and aspirations.

Now the time had come for the all-important resolution. Ralph Abernathy read the words slowly and forcefully. The main substance of the resolution called upon the Negroes not to resume riding the buses until (1) courteous treatment by the bus operators was guaranteed; (2) passengers were seated on a first-come, first-served basis—Negroes sitting from the back of the bus toward the front while whites were seated from the front towards the back; (3) Negro bus operators were employed on predominantly Negro routes. At the words "All in favor of the motion stand," every person stood up, and those who were already standing raised their hands. Cheers began to ring out from both inside and outside. The motion was carried unanimously. The people had expressed their determination not to ride the buses until conditions were changed.

At the point I had to leave the meeting and rush to the other side of town to speak at a YMCA banquet. As I drove away my heart was full. I had never seen such enthusiasm for freedom. And yet this enthusiasm was tempered by amazing self-discipline. The unity of purpose and esprit de corps of these people had been indescribably moving. No historian would ever be able fully to describe this meeting and no sociologist would ever be able to interpret it adequately. One had to be a part of the experience really to understand it.

At the Ben Moore Hotel, as the elevator slowly moved up to the roof garden where the banquet was being held, I said to myself, the victory is already won, no matter how long we struggle to attain the three points of the resolution. It is a victory infinitely larger than the bus situation. The real victory was in the mass meeting, where thousands of black people stood revealed with a new sense of dignity and destiny.

Many will inevitably raise the question, why did this event take place in Montgomery, Alabama, in 1955? Some have suggested that the Supreme Court decision on school desegregation, handed down less than two years before, had given new hope of eventual justice to Negroes everywhere, and fired them with the necessary spark of encouragement to rise against their oppression. But although this might help to explain why the protest occurred when it did it cannot explain why it happened in Montgomery.

Certainly,there is a partial explanation in the long history of injustice on the buses of Montgomery. The bus protest did not spring into being full grown as Athena sprang from the head of Zeus; it was the culmination of a slowly developing process. Mrs Parks' arrest was the precipitating factor rather than the cause of the protest. The cause lay deep in the record of similar injustices. Almost everybody could point to an unfortunate episode that he himself had experienced or seen.

But there comes a time when people get tried of being trampled by oppression. There comes a time when people get tired of being plunged into the abyss of exploitation and nagging injustice. The story of Montgomery is the story of 50,000 such Negroes who were willing to substitute tired feet for tired souls,and walk the street of Montgomery until the walls of segregation were finally battered by the forces of justice.

But neither is this the whole explanation. Negroes in other communities confronted conditions equally as bad and often worse. So we cannot explain the Montgomery story merely in terms of the abuses that Negroes suffered there. Moreover, it cannot be explained by a pre-existent unity among the leaders, since we have seen that Montgomery Negro community prior to the protest was marked by divided leadership, indifference, and complacency. Nor can it be explained by the appearance upon the scene of new leadership. The Montgomery story would have taken place if the leaders of the protest had never been born.

So every rational explanation breaks down at some point. There is something about the protest that is supra-rational; it cannot be explained without a divine dimension. Some may call it a principle of concretion, with Alfred N. Whitehead; or a process of integration, with Henry N. Wiseman; or Being-itself,with Paul Tillich; or a personal God. Whatever the name, some extra-human force labors to create a harmony out of the discords of the universe. There is a creative power that works to pull down mountains of evil and level hilltops of injustice. God still works through history His wonders to perform. It seems as though God had decided to use Montgomery as the proving ground for the struggle and triumph of freedom and justice in America. And what better place for it than the leading symbol of the Old South? It is one of the splendid ironies of our day that Montgomery, the Cradle of the Confederacy, is being transformed into Montgomery, the Cradle of Freedom and Justice.

The day of days, Monday, December 5, 1955, was drawing to a close. We all prepared to go to our homes, not yet fully aware of what had happened. The deliberations of that brisk, cool night in December will not be forgotten. That night we were starting a movement that would gain national recognition; whose echoes would ring in the ears of people of every nation; a movement that would astound the oppressor, and bring new hope to the oppressed. That night was Montgomery's moment in history.

ANNEXURE 10

(Quoted from M.K. Baruah, *Portrait of a Gandhian: Biography of Dr. Martin Luther King Jr.*, Gauhati, 1985, p.33)

On September 17, 1958, King published his first book, *Strides Toward Freedom.* Under the terms of his contract, he was required to make public appearances in several northern cities. He was in Detroit and in Chicago at first. In both these cities he spoke to large friendly crowds. But the Black Nationalists did not approve of the principles espoused in his book: the doctrine of love.

Next, King went to New York, where in a Harlem department store, he sat in the shoe section to autograph his book. Hundreds of people, seeking autographs, encircled King. Among the crowd was a middle-aged woman who was anxiously pushing towards King. "Is that Martin Luther King," the woman asked a department store employee, who replied: "Yes it is." Still pushing herself forward, the woman addressing King, asked "Are you Mr. King?" and he replied, "Yes I am". "I've been after you for five years," she said. Then with loud curses the woman thrust a sharp letter opener in the left side of King's chest. Pandemonium ignited in the crowded department store, as the crazed woman was still attacking him with blows and curses. Finally, a few onlookers overcame the woman, and held her for the police. The wounded King was rushed through the hysteric crowd to the Harlem Hospital.

King's attacker, a 42 year old woman, who was born in Georgia but who lived half her life in New York City, gave the city police several incoherent versions of motives for her actions. First, she accused people for torturing her. Then she alleged that Dr. King was trying to convert her from Roman Catholicism, and yet in another breath, she said that she was an anti-integrationist. So she wanted to kill King because he was the leader of the NAACP. She also told the police that she was glad for what she did.

In Harlem Hospital, a team of doctors removed the letter opener from King's chest. To reach the wound, the surgeon had to remove a part of one of King's rib. After the three hour operation, King was placed on the critical list.

Mrs. King, who was in Montgomery at that time, rushed to New York to be with her husband. He was almost a sneeze away from certain death. According to Dr. Emil A. Naclerio, one of the surgeons who performed the operations, the sharp tip of the letter opener's blade had penetrated to the outer wall of King's aorta. Dr. Naclerio conjectured that if King had sneezed or coughed, the blade would have entered the aorta, the main arterial trunk from the heart.

The news of Dr. King's attempted assassination spread over the country. A large crowd of his admirers gathered outside the hospital, as messages and flowers poured in from well wishers and prominent national political leaders.

Meanwhile the messages and flowers began to pour in from many parts of the country. Governor Averell Harriman who was campaigning for reelection in New York city, paid a visit to King. Vice President Nixon sent a message. Many religious groups and organisations such as the Inter-racial Ministerial Alliances, the Crew of the SS. America, sent messages and flowers. King was buoyant with the love and affection of well-wishers during his period of convalescence. Mrs. King was near him all the time. King had already attained national prominence then. So many important persons visited him during his stay at the hospital.

The next day after the incident, Izola Curry, the accused woman, was arraigned before Magistrate Vincent Roo. "I understand, this is the woman accused of stabbing the Reverend King with a knife," Roo commented. Curry corrected the Magistrate, "No, it was a letter opener." Assistant

District Attorney Howard Jones said to the Magistrate at this point, "I would like her held without bail."

Mrs. Curry, the deranged woman, again said, "I am charging him as well as he is charging me." "What have you got against him?" the Magistrate asked. "I am charging him with being mixed up with the communists. I have reported the case to the FBI and it is being looked into," the woman said. "This woman is ill," Magistrate Roo declared. Magistrate Roo ordered a psychiatric examination of Mrs. Curry. Mrs. Curry objected, but at any rate she was committed to Bellevue Hospital psychiatric ward for mental examination. Then, she was committed to the Mathewan State Hospital for the criminally insane.

ANNEXURE 11
(Quoted from S.K. Biswas, *Dr. Ambedkar and the Constitution of India*)

On 25th November, 1949, on the floor of Central Hall of the Parliament of India, in the front rank, Dr. Ambedkar took his stand before the full view of that august galaxy and started in his articulated confirmity:

> Looking back on the work of the Constituent Assembly it will now be two years, eleven months and seventeen days since it first met on the 9th of December, 1946. During this period the Constituent Assembly has altogether held eleven sessions. Out of these eleven sessions, the first six were spent in passing the Objectives Resolution and the consideration of the Reports of Committees on Fundamental Rights, on Union Constitution, on Union Powers, on Provincial Constitution, on Minorities and on the Scheduled Areas and Scheduled Tribes. The seventh, eight, ninth, tenth and the eleventh sessions were devoted to the consideration of the Draft Constitution. These eleven sessions of the Constituent Assembly have consumed 165 days. Out of these, the Assembly spent 114 days for the consideration of the Draft Constitution. Coming to the Drafting Committee, it was elected by the Constituent Assembly on 29th August 1947. It held its first meeting on 30th August. Since August 30th it sat for 141 days during which it was engaged in the preparation of the Draft Constitution. The Draft Constitution, as prepared by the Constitutional Adviser as a text for the Drafting Committee to work upon, consisted of 243 Articles and 13 Schedules. The first Draft Constitution as presented by the Drafting Committee to the Constituent Assembly contained 315 Articles and 8 Schedules. At the end of the consideration stage, the number of Articles in the Draft Constitution increased to 386 Articles and 8 Schedules. The total number of amendments to the Draft Constitution tabled was approximately 7,635. Of them, the total number of amendments actually moved in the house were 2,473.

The great heart also disclosed his expectation and achievements with all politeness:

> I came into the Constituent Assembly with no greater aspiration than to safeguard the interests of the Scheduled Castes. I had not the remotest idea that I would be called upon to undertake more responsible functions. I was therefore, greatly surprised when the Assembly elected me to the Drafting Committee. I was more than surprised when the Drafting Committee elected me to be its Chairman. There were in the Drafting Committee men bigger, better and more competent than myself, sush as my friend Sir Alladi Krishnaswami Iyer. I am grateful to the Constituent Assembly and the Drafting Committee for reposing in me so much trust and confidence and to have chosen me as their instrument and given me this opportunity of serving the country.

Now, the question remains, how this angry untouchable Mahar could have got his entry into this luminious galaxy to decide on the instrumentalities of India? The nut-shell history of that is as follows.

Dr. Ambedkar was called in the Simon Commission to give evidence and he put his impressive mark in the process of framing the Constitution future India was to have. He was then invited to attend the Round Table Conference in London in 1930, 31, and 32. All the sessions he attended to finalise the Government of India Act, 1935. Dr. Ambedkar was appointed as a member of the Executive Counsel of Viceroy as Labour Member on 6th June, 1942.

The Hindu chauvinism compelled him to seek his candidature from Bengal. With the help of Muslim League, Government of Bengal the untouchables of Bengal, however, succeed to return Dr. Ambedkar in the Constituent Assembly with maximum votes in the first quarter of 1946.

But his membership became void on 15th August 1947, only eight months after the first meet of the Constituent

Assembly on 9th December, 1946, because those who voted him to the Assembly became foreigners, the citizens of East Pakistan. At this juncture it was National Congress who got Dr. Ambedkar returned from a Bombay seat, created with the resignation of Mr. Joyakar. Dr. Ambedkar became a member for the second time. And the entire establishment became eager to use his invaluable services. Things happened very rapidly. As if the then national leaders ran after Dr. Ambedkar to lure him to give his service to the nation.

On a Good Friday he ceased to be a member of the Constituent Assembly and before the next friday came he not only became the member of the Constituent Assembly once again, but he was also born as a member of the Committee to consider Independence Act, etc. Let us witness the incident.

Almost abruptly, Dr. Rajendra Parsad, adjourned the proceedings on 20th August and declared:

> There will be further discussion tomorrow about this.
>
> Before we adjourn, I desire to make an announcement. A Committee consisting of Mr. Mavalankar, Mr. Hussain Imam, Shri Purushottamdas Tandon, Dr. Ambedkar, Mr. Alladi Krishnaswami Ayyar, Mr. Gopalaswami Ayyangar and Mr. B.L. Mitter is appointed to consider the Indian Independence Act, the adaptations of the Government of India Act, 1935, the Rules and Standing Orders of the Legislative Assembly, the Rules and Standing Orders in force in the Constituent Assembly, etc. and report on the following matters:
>
> (1) What are the precise functions of the Constituent Assembly under the Indian Independence Act?
>
> (2) Is it possible to distinguish between the business of the Constituent Assembly as a Constitution-making body and its other business and can the Constituent Assembly set apart certain days or periods solely for the former?
>
> (3) Should the members representing the Indian States in the Constituent Assembly be given the right to take part in

proceedings which do not relate to constitution-making or to the subjects in respect of which they have acceded?

(4) What new rules or standing orders, if any, and what amendments if any in the existing Rules or Standing Orders should be made by the Constituent Assembly or its Presidents.

It was none but Dr. Ambedkar who submitted the report of this "Constituent Assembly Functions Committee" on 29th August, 1947.

Mr. President, I beg to move that this Assembly proceed to take into consideration the Report on the functions of the Constituent Assembly under the Indian Independence Act, 1947, submitted by the Committee appointed by the President in pursuance of the Decisions of the Assembly on the 20th August 1947.

Altogether the Committee has made five recommendations. Its fourth recommendation is that (4) the work of the Constituent Assembly as a Constitution-making body and as an ordinary legislature should be separated and should be conducted in separate sessions to be held on separate days.

The resolution also was adopted. The record of the Constituent Assembly Debates, Vol. 5 dated 29th August, 1947 holds:

That the Resolution as a whole be adopted, namely:

1. That with reference to the Motion by the Honourable Dr. B.R. Ambedkar regarding the consideration of the Report on the functions of the Constituent Assembly under the Indian Independence Act, it is hereby resolved that

(i) The functions of the Assembly shall be -

(a) to continue and complete the work of Constitution-making which commenced on 9th December, 1946 and to function as the Dominion Legislature until a Legislature under the new Constitution comes into being.

On this day the Assembly also decided to constitute the Committee to draft the Constitution of India. The records reveal as follows:

> The Constituent Assembly of India on August 29, 1947 adopted a resolution authorising the appointment of a Drafting Committee to scrutinise the draft of the text of the Constitution of India prepared by the constitutional Adviser, giving effect to the decisions taken already in the Assembly and including all matters which are ancillary thereto or which have to be provided in such a Constitution, and to submit to the Assembly for consideration the text of the draft constitution as revised by the Committee.

The committee consisted of seven members namely, Alladi Krishnaswami Ayyar, N. Gopalaswami Ayyangar, B.R. Ambedkar, K.M. Munshi, Muhammad Saadulla, B.L. Mitter and D.P. Kaitan. In case any of the members was unable to attend any meeting or if there arose a vacancy, the President was authorised to make necessary arrangements. B.L. Mitter was unable to attend any of its meetings after the first sitting of the Drafting Committee as he ceased to be a member of the Constituent Assembly. N. Madhava Rao was nominated on December 5, 1947 by the President in his place.

In its maiden meeting, next day, 30th August the Drafting Committee unanimously elected none but Dr. Ambedkar as Chairman of the Committee. From 27th onwards Dr. Ambedkar called regular meetings to complete the draft of the Constitution of India. In all in 44 meetings he completed his job and handed over the draft Constitution in the benign hands of the Honourable President of the Constituent Assembly of India. In the forwarding letter dated 21st February, 1948 he observed:

> Introductory: On behalf of the Drafting Committee appointed by the resolution of the Constituent Assembly of

> August 29, 1947, I submit herewith the Draft of the new Constitution of India as settled by the committee.
>
> Although I have been authorised to sign the Draft on behalf of the members of the committee, I should make it clear that not all the members were present at all the meetings of the committee. But at every meeting at which any decision was taken the necessary quorum was present and the decisions were either unanimous or by a majority of those present.
>
> In preparing the Draft the Drafting Committee was of course expected to follow the decisions taken by the Constituent Assembly or by the various committees appointed by the Constituent Assembly. This the Drafting Committee has endeavoured to do as far as possible. There are, however, some matters in respect of which the Drafting Committee felt it necessary to suggest certain changes...
>
> A separate note recorded by Shri Alladi Krishnaswami Ayyar on certain points (not involving any question of principle), is appended to the Draft at his request.
>
> I cannot transmit to you this Draft Constitution without placing on record the Committee's gratitude for the assistance the committee has received in this difficult task from Sri B.N. Rau, the Constitutional Adviser, Shri S.K. Mukerjee, Joint Secretary and Draftsman, and the staff of the Constituent Assembly Secretariat.

Many scholars have failed to note that there is an immeasurable gap between a Constitutional Advisor and the authority in the Chairman or a Member of the Drafting Committee.

Once again, in his speech, while introducing the Draft Constitution in the Constituent Assembly of India on 4th November, 1948 called often by the President, Honourable Dr. Rajendra Prasad, in the Chair, Dr. Ambedkar concluded:

> But this I would like to say. The Constitution has been discussed in some of the Provincial Assemblies of India. It was discussed in Bombay, C.P., West Bengal, Bihar, Madras and East Punjab. It is true that in some Provincial Assemblies serious objections were taken to the financial provisions of the Constitution and in Madras to Article 226. But excepting this, in no Provincial Assembly has any serious objection taken to the Articles of the Constitution. No Constitution is perfect and the Drafting Committee itself is suggesting certain amendments to improve the Draft Constitution. But the Debates in the Provincial Assemblies give me courage to say that the Constitution as settled by the Drafting Committee is good enough to... start with. I feel that it is workable, it is flexible and it is strong enough to hold the country together both in peace-time and in war-time. Indeed, if I may say so, if things go wrong under the new Constitution, the reason will not be that we had a bad Constitution. What we will have to say is the Man was vile...

If we analyse the services rendered by the other members of the Draft Committee to the Chairman Dr. Ambedkar in framing the Draft we find a very disappointing picture. While finalising the instrumentalities of our Nation which was to go down through the millenniums, the members refrained even to attend its meetings numbering 44 only. The maximum meetings were attended by the Muslim Member Janab Sadulah, he attended 32 meetings. Sri Krishna Ayyar attended 29, Madhava Rao 28, K.M. Munshi 27, Ayyangar 16, Kaitan three meetings. In January 1948 there took place only eleven meetings; out of these on seven meetings there was only one member present with the Chairman; he was Shri Madhava Rao.

Index